HOW ATTACHMENT STYLES WORK

Discover The Cause Of Your Relationship Patterns & Learn To Build Love That Lasts

689 Burke Rd
Camberwell Victoria 3124
Australia

www.LearnWellBooks.com

We're led by God. Our business is also committed to supporting kids' charities. At the time of printing, we have donated well over $100,000 to enable mentoring services for underprivileged children. By choosing our books, you are helping children who desperately need it. Thank you.

This is really important.
It's a sincere thank you.

My name is Wayne, the founder of LearnWell.

My Dad put a book in my hands when I was 13. It was written by Zig Ziglar and it changed the course of my life. Since then, it's been books that have helped me get over breakups, learn how to be a good friend, study the lives of good people and books have been the source of my persistence through some pretty challenging times.

My purpose is now to return the favor. To create books that might be the turning point in the lives of people around the world, just like they've been for me. It's enough to almost bring me to tears to think of you holding this book, seeking information and wisdom from something that I've helped to create. I'm moved in a way that I can't fully explain.

We're a small and 'beyond-enthusiastic' team here at LearnWell. We're writers, editors, researchers, designers, formatters (oh … and a bookkeeper!) who take your decision to learn with us incredibly seriously. We consider it a privilege to be part of your learning journey. Thank you for allowing us to join you.

If there's anything we did really well, anything we messed up, or anything AT ALL that we could do better, would you please write to us and tell us (like, right now!) We would love to hear from you!

readers@learnwellbooks.com

We're sending you our thanks, our love and our very best wishes.

Wayne

and the team at LearnWell Books.

LearnWell Books

At LearnWell, we think learning is the most important thing a person can do. Learners grow, lead, and solve important problems. We consider it a privilege that you've chosen one of our books to learn from.

In return, we have invested significant effort in creating what we believe are the best books in the world, on the topics we choose to write about.

Your book comes with several complementary features, including:

WORKBOOK

Accompanying this book is a comprehensive Workbook that will enhance your learning and increase your knowledge retention.

Before reading, please get your copy of the Workbook here:

www.learnwellbooks.com/secure

It contains exercises that match the content of each chapter. It's interactive, user-friendly and proven to be the best way to absorb the valuable information in this book.

EMAIL LEARNING COURSE

As we write our books, we conduct enormous amounts of research. Not all of what we discover ends up in the books but some of this information is highly relevant and deserves to be shared. So, our writers capture these interesting 'side-notes' in a series of short emails. These messages become like a private tutorial. Similar to having the writer sitting with you as you read, sharing their thoughts and insights.

If you choose to get the Workbook, you will also be entitled to receive this online tutorial, at no charge.

To Kate

If only I knew this then

CONTENTS

WORKBOOK

The average reader remembers just 14% of what they read. To dramatically enhance the amount of knowledge you absorb on this important topic, we have produced a user-friendly Workbook that follows the content of this book, chapter by chapter. Before beginning this book, make sure you receive a copy of your Workbook. Follow the link below:

Get Access To Your Free Workbook Here:

www.learnwellbooks.com/secure

INTRODUCTION

Welcome to a transformative journey of self-discovery and relationship growth. In this book, we will embark on a profound exploration of attachment theory and its impact on your relationships. Prepare to gain a thorough understanding of your relationship patterns, emotional responses, and deeply ingrained behaviors.

Chapter by chapter, we will delve into the core aspects of attachment theory and its practical application. Together, we will uncover the reasons why your relationships may have followed familiar patterns and discover how to break free from those that you no longer wish to repeat..

In our quest for understanding, we will explore the genesis of your attachment style and its connection to your early-life experiences. By identifying your unique attachment style, whether it is secure, anxious, avoidant, or disorganized, we will unravel the intricacies of your interactions with others.

With each chapter, we will learn more about the characteristics, challenges, and coping mechanisms associated with each attachment style. We will examine secure attachment, often considered the healthiest way of relating to others, as well as the specific dynamics of avoidant, anxious, and disorganized attachment styles.

But this journey isn't just about knowledge; it's about transformation. To facilitate your growth, we have included a comprehensive

Workbook. This practical tool will guide you in applying the concepts discussed in each chapter, empowering you to create healthier, more fulfilling relationships. We suggest you get your copy of the Workbook before you commence the first chapter. You'll find that here: www.learnwellbooks.com/secure

As we progress, you will develop self-awareness, learning how to revolutionize your relationships and attract the love you deserve. We will explore the essential skills of effective communication, emotional regulation, setting boundaries, and healing attachment wounds.

Throughout this book, we encourage you to approach your personal growth with patience, courage, and consistent effort. Change takes time, but with dedication, you can create lasting transformations in your life. By the end of this journey, our goal is for you to view yourself and others with compassion, armed with the knowledge and tools to forge stronger, more meaningful connections.

Get ready to unravel the intricate workings of your relationships, gain clarity, and build a future filled with love, understanding, and fulfillment. The path to healthier relationships starts here.

WHY ALL YOUR RELATIONSHIPS END UP THE SAME

Reassurance, Resilience, Refocus, Reprogram

Human beings are a species evolved for secure connection with others, that's just human biology & neuroscience. But some of us wonder if we can feel secure without being abandoned & some of us wonder if we can feel secure without being overwhelmed. Some of us a little of both.[1]

— *Allyson Dinneen*

ATTACHED OR DETACHED?

Imagine waking up to the sound of soothing rain tapping against your window in your small one-bedroom apartment. As you stretch your limbs and rouse yourself to full consciousness, your hand reaches out to the empty space beside you, seeking the comfort of your loved one. They aren't there. Confused, you sit up and survey the room. A sudden jolt of alarm grips you as your eyes sweep across the room, and you realize that numerous articles of their clothing are missing from the closet. Unnerved, you rush to the living room where you discover your partner preoccupied with packing their belongings. Panic sets in as you realize what's happening. Tears stream down your face as you plead with them not to leave. You beg them to stay and work through whatever problems you're facing, but they're unresponsive.

Laura had long been plagued by anxiety when it came to matters of the heart. Her attachment style was anxious, an insatiable need for constant attention and reassurance from her partner. Alex, on the other hand, possessed an avoidant attachment style, making it nearly impossible for him to open up emotionally and form deep connections with others. This fundamental discord had created a great deal of strain between them, and it seemed that Alex had finally hit his limit. As the reality of his departure settled in, Laura's anxiety reached new heights. The loss of him felt like a part of her would be forever lost. She couldn't fathom life without him. The memories of her past traumas and losses flooded her mind, rendering the breakup an intolerable anguish. Why did no one have the strength to love her? It wasn't the first or second time she'd been confronted with this incomprehensible agony.

Alex's voice finally broke the suffocating silence, and he revealed to her his need for space, to find some clarity about their future. He expressed that continuing their relationship in its current form was untenable. For Laura, it was as if her most profound apprehensions had been ratified, solidifying her belief that she was fundamentally unworthy of love. The weight of her anxiety swelled with the sight of Alex departing from their apartment, abandoning her to face her mounting fears and insecurities in solitude.

Laura had been down this road before. A familiar cycle of anxiety and avoidance that seemed to follow her from one relationship to the next. It was like a broken record, each time playing out the same way.

In college, she had met Ryan, her first serious boyfriend. He was more emotionally distant than she was used to, which only made her more anxious. She craved reassurance, but his lack of response only fed her insecurities.

Their relationship had ended when Ryan had grown tired of her constant neediness and had broken up with her. Laura was left feeling devastated and alone, vowing never to be so clingy again.

But old habits die hard, and in her subsequent relationships, Laura found herself falling back into the same patterns of behavior. She would become increasingly anxious as her partner grew more distant, creating a vicious cycle of insecurity and avoidance.

There came a point with Alex when she was determined to break the cycle. She knew that her anxious attachment style was causing him to become more avoidant, and she didn't want to lose him.

It was time for her to take responsibility for her own issues with attachment and work towards becoming a more secure partner.

However, it's worth noting that modifying behavior to accommodate attachment styles is not always successful. It can be a delicate dance, and sometimes one partner's attempts at reassurance can trigger the other's anxieties or avoidance. Often, it takes both people in a relationship to accommodate the other's attachment style in order for it to work.

For example, there was a time when Laura had a family emergency and needed support from Alex. She reached out to him, hoping for comfort and reassurance, but Alex, feeling overwhelmed by the intensity of her emotions, withdrew and became distant. Her grandmother, who she had been very close to, was sick and in the hospital. Grief gripped her as she sat in the cold and depressing hospital, staring at her phone. It was a time when she should be tending to her loving grandmother, not glued to her phone waiting for a text! She couldn't understand how he could abandon her at this time. For Alex, confronting loss in any form was too painful. He wasn't prepared to extend any form of sympathy to Laura as he couldn't always comprehend it in his own life. Laura felt hurt, and the incident only served to exacerbate her anxieties.

One particular moment where Alex felt *his* needs were unmet in their relationship was when he longed for more personal space and time alone to work on his art practice, but Laura struggled to give him that. She had a habit of constantly checking in on him throughout the day and bombarding him with texts. To Laura, this was a measure to see how much Alex still cared about her in moments when she was feeling insecure. This would often have the opposite effect, and would overwhelm Alex and make him feel trapped.

After feeling suffocated, Alex finally decided to talk to Laura about his concerns. He expressed his appreciation for their relationship but also acknowledged his need for solitude, hoping that they could work together to find a compromise. However, Laura was hurt by his request, thinking that he no longer wanted to spend time with her. She took it personally. Her feelings led her to become defensive, which caused the conversation to escalate into an argument, leaving both of them feeling unheard and frustrated.

On the other hand, Laura also had her own set of unmet needs in the relationship. She yearned for more affection and reassurance from Alex, but he found it challenging to provide that, often withdrawing or appearing emotionally distant.

One day, Laura summoned the courage to open up to Alex about her insecurities. She expressed her gratitude for him but also asked for more emotional connection, hoping he could be more affectionate and communicative with her. Unfortunately, Alex reacted defensively, thinking that he was being criticized for something he couldn't control. As a result, the conversation turned into another argument, and both parties failed to understand each other's needs, leading to a breakdown in communication.

This episode shows how both Alex and Laura struggled to communicate their needs, leading to misunderstandings and a lack of empathy towards one another. It emphasizes the importance of honest and open communication in a relationship, as well as the willingness to listen and compromise. Most of all, it shows the need for both partners to reach deep within their histories, traumas, and personality traits, in order to seek change.

DEPENDENCY PARADOX

In the depths of her despair, Laura recalled one evening. Alex and Laura had planned a night out with friends. As they were getting ready, Laura began to feel anxious about being in a large group of people she didn't know very well. She turned to Alex and expressed her worries, hoping for some reassurance.

Alex put a hand on her shoulder and looked into her eyes. "I'm here for you," he said. "You don't have to be afraid. I'll be by your side the whole time."

Laura felt a wave of relief wash over her. She knew she could depend on Alex to be there for her, and that made her feel more confident and secure. As they arrived at the party and started mingling, Laura found herself feeling more comfortable and at ease than she expected.

Later that night, as they were walking home, Laura turned to Alex and thanked him for being there for her. "I don't know what I would do without you," she said. Alex smiled and took her hand. "I'm always here for you, Laura. You can depend on me."

In that moment, Laura realized that by depending on Alex, she was able to develop her own sense of independence. Knowing that she had a secure base to rely on allowed her to explore the world with more confidence and courage. And she knew that no matter what, Alex would always be there for her.

WHAT CONTRIBUTED TO THEIR ATTACHMENT STYLES?

Laura's childhood experiences deeply affected her attachment style in relationships. In her youth, Laura experienced the stark realities of emotional neglect, stemming from her parents' erratic and inattentive style of child-rearing. Her mother, working arduous hours to keep the family afloat, had little time to devote to Laura and her younger brother. Meanwhile, her father's dependency on alcohol left him emotionally distant and unavailable.

The lack of consistent care and affection in her early years left Laura with a deep-seated need for attention and validation. This need, rooted in her formative experiences, spilled over into her romantic relationships, causing her to become anxious and clingy with her partners. Among the moments etched into her memory was a particularly harrowing incident when she was only ten. Her father had gone missing for days on end, and with her mother working a double shift, Laura was left to look after her younger brother. Despite her attempts to reach out, she was unable to locate her father and when she tried to contact her mother's workplace, was met with the crushing news that her mother was too occupied to speak with her.

For Laura, this experience became a catalyst for her desperate search for constant affirmation and attention, as she did not wish to be left alone and vulnerable again. This would play a critical role in her attachment style, where she always yearned for assurance and validation from her partners, as she struggled to find it within herself. The emotional neglect from her childhood had a lasting impact on her attachment style and the way she formed relationships.

As a child, Alex experienced a traumatic event that led to his development of an avoidant attachment style. When he was six years old, he witnessed his parents go through a messy divorce. The process was emotionally draining for Alex, as he felt like he was caught in the middle of their constant fighting and arguments.

In that tumultuous time, Alex found himself at the center of his parents' fights, used as a bargaining chip in their emotional warfare. Amidst the bickering and bantering, he felt adrift in a sea of confusion and uncertainty, unsure of where to turn or whom to trust. The constant tug-of-war for his affection left him feeling like a puppet on strings, forever walking on eggshells to avoid upsetting either side.

The divorce, too, left its mark on Alex's tender heart, forcing him to spend time away from his mother, his primary caregiver. He yearned for his father's embrace, but stifled his emotions, afraid of causing his mother any more pain. It was a time of self-imposed solitude and stoicism, as he learned to bottle up his feelings and prioritize self-reliance above all else.

This traumatic experience led to Alex's development of an avoidant attachment style. He learned to keep his emotions to himself and avoid getting too close to others, as he didn't want to be hurt or caught in the middle of their conflicts. He believed that emotional detachment was the best way to protect himself from the pain and confusion of interpersonal relationships.

MOVING AHEAD

In the following weeks, Laura struggled to come to terms with the dissolution of her relationship. She was consumed by an immobilizing despair, unable to disentangle herself from the bed as the world swirled around her. Her anxious attachment style made it all the more difficult for her to acknowledge and accept that the relationship had come to an end, and she was persistently plagued by thoughts of what could have been. How she may have behaved differently toward Alex. Nevertheless, she recognized that to have more productive and fulfilling relationships in the future, she would need to devote time and energy to better comprehending herself.

Laura knew that the road ahead would be challenging, but she was ready to put in the work. She was determined to break the cycle once and for all, and to finally find the love and security she so desperately craved.

As for Alex, his avoidant attachment style impeded his ability to fully confront and deal with the breakup in a healthy manner. He buried himself in work and steered clear of anything that might trigger reminders of their past, choosing to sidestep the underlying issues that precipitated their separation..

In the end, their opposing attachment styles proved insurmountable, and they were forced to go their separate ways. The experience was acutely distressing for both parties, but it also presented an opportunity for self-reflection and personal growth, provided they were willing to seize it.

YOUR OWN ATTACHMENT STYLE

In this book, we will explore relationships and attachment styles like Alex and Laura's. If you've found yourself entangled in the messy throes of uncertain relational dynamics, fear not. You and I will begin to find a path forward. We will examine communication issues or misunderstandings that contribute to the breakdown of relationships. We will look at how past experiences and traumas shape attachment styles and behavior in relationships. We'll explore how one person's behavior can trigger the other person's attachment style, creating a cycle of insecurity and avoidance. We will also examine whether changing one's behavior to accommodate the other person's attachment style is successful or unsuccessful. We will consider whether either person feels like their needs are not being met in the relationship and how they communicate this to their partner. Of utmost significance is the self-assessment that will aid us in establishing your unique attachment style. By doing so, you will be equipped with the tools necessary to apply the knowledge contained within this book in a manner that best suits your individual requirements.

ATTACHMENT STYLES

As grown-ups, we've all formed connections with others, be they platonic or romantic, familial or friendly. These relationships are dynamic and can change in unforeseeable ways, leaving us feeling powerless. There are multiple methods of attachment, each unique in its own right. First, we have secure attachments, the hallmark of successful and healthy relationships. This is the type of attachment we shall strive towards in this book. Second, there are avoidant attachments, exemplified by Alex's withdrawn and inhibited demeanor. Third, we have anxious attachments, as seen in the pained heart of Laura above. Fourth, disorganized attachment styles can emerge in individuals due to a combination of attachment styles, which can lead to confusion and uncertainty.

Attachments are an essential part of life, providing meaning and depth to our experiences. The goal of this book is to enable you to comprehend your attachment style, as well as that of your loved ones. With this knowledge, you will be equipped to navigate the different attachment styles, and work towards achieving a secure attachment.

The following are ten indicators of secure attachment in adult relationships:

- Effective management of emotions and feelings within the relationship

- Demonstrating strong self-directed behavior when not in a relationship

- Skilled at establishing emotional connections, being vulnerable and trusting others

- Having clarity of purpose and direction in life

- Proficient in communicating one's needs effectively

- Feeling a sense of agency and impact in the world around them

- At ease with intimacy and mutual dependence in relationships

- Seeking emotional support from their partner and providing support in return

- Comfortable with solitude and utilizing that time for self-exploration

- Possessing a strong ability to reflect on their actions within the relationship[2]

Turn now to your Workbook and begin to create a foundation of understanding of your participation in your own relationships. There are prompts to guide your reflections.

When you've finished that, chapter two will help you discover the science and reasoning behind how all of these varying attachment styles have come about!

2

HOW
ATTACHMENT
THEORY WORKS

... And Why It May Be The Answer
To Your Relationship Problems

*Healing takes courage, and we all have courage,
even if we have to dig a little to find it.*

– Tori Amos

Have you ever stopped to ponder why certain individuals have an innate ability to forge profound, soul-stirring relationships with ease, while others find themselves in a constant state of disconnection? The answer can be traced back to the pioneering research of attachment theory, a framework that sparked a revolution in the realm of psychology, forever altering our perception of the intricacies of human bonds. In this chapter, we'll get to know the history of attachment theory, unearthing how this concept can be your ticket to cultivating more robust, gratifying relationships. We'll start with the role of your childhood and the way your caregivers (.e. Your parents or whoever took care of you as a baby) may have played a part in forming your attachment style.

John Bowlby (1907-1990) was a man with a mission: he wanted to shine more light on child psychiatry. He had a front-row seat to the trials and tribulations of the human psyche, thanks to his work at a psychiatric hospital. As one of attachment theory's founding fathers, he aimed to challenge the status quo of psychoanalytic thought and offer a fresh perspective on the roots of separation-related anxiety.

66 *"We learn our belief systems as very little children, and then we move through life creating experiences to match our beliefs. Look back in your own life and notice how often you have gone through the same experience."* 99
– John Bowlby

Bowlby's hypothesis suggested that attachment wasn't just a social construct, but rather a deeply ingrained biological mechanism linking a child to their primary caregiver—usually a parent. This behavior-driven mechanism ensures that the child remains close to their caregiver, upping their survival chances and keeping them out of harm's way. So remember, you're not some irreparably damaged being—you're simply a product of circumstance and science, things you had no control over. But now, it's time to delve into what shaped you or your loved one into who you are today.

But first, we must talk about Mary Ainsworth (1913-1999). Ainsworth was a Candadian developmental psychologist and known to be the second founder of Attachment Theory.[3] She devised the "Strange Situation" experiment, a psychological version of musical chairs. But in this game, when the music stops, it reveals how a child explores and interacts with their world, all based on that parent-child bond. If Bowlby and Ainsworth were watchmakers, they'd be masters of their craft. Bowlby forged the watch's inner gears, explaining why babies stick to their parents like magnets to a fridge. It's not just social - it's biology, survival. It's like the sun rising and setting each day, as predictable and natural as it gets.

Through this experiment, Ainsworth uncovered valuable insights into the intricate interplay between an infant's attachment style and their propensity to explore the world around them. It remains a cornerstone of research in the field of attachment theory to this day. It's like understanding your daily routine is influenced by the rhythm of that sun we talked about - rising, setting, and everything in between. Predictable, yet intriguing. So, dear reader, get ready. We're about to rewind your watch and discover why it ticks the way it does.[4]

The Strange Situation Study was designed to observe an infant's exploration behavior with their mother and in her absence, as well as in the presence of a stranger. Through this experiment, the foundation for an attachment classification system was established, enabling the differentiation between a child's ambivalent and dismissing behaviors when reunited with their mother. This experiment provided a unique window into attachment behaviors and paved the way for a deeper understanding of the complex dynamics that shape our earliest relationships.[5,6]

Researchers watched 100 middle class American families' 12 to 18-month-old children in a room through a one-way mirror. The room was filled with toys and the child was initially with their mother. The Strange Situation experiment involved eight 3-minute steps.[7]

1. Mother and infant alone.

2. A stranger enters the room.

3. The mother leaves the baby and stranger alone.

4. The mother returns.

5. The stranger leaves.

6. The mother leaves and the child is left alone.

7. The stranger returns.

8. Mother returns and the stranger exits.[8]

From The Strange Situation experiment Ainsworth established the Strange Situation Classification (SSC), which is the basis of our current understanding of attachment styles. Ainsworth's classification system identified distinct attachment styles, each with their unique set of behaviors and characteristics.

Secure – When separated from the mother, the child exhibits signs of distress, but can be comforted quickly and returns to a positive state upon reuniting with them.

Anxious – When the mother departs, the child exhibits a high level of distress, but upon their return, the child resists contact with them despite their distress.

Avoidant – The child appears to show no signs of distress upon separation from their mother and does not appear interested in their mother's return.[9]

Disorganized – These children behave in a puzzling manner that combines perplexity, disorientation, and acting bewildered. They could show their parents resistance or avoidance.

> *"Secure attachment is associated with the capacity to follow another person's state of mind and is the basis of social understanding and meaningful social relations."*
> *– Peter Fonagy*

Diving into the world of attachment as a biological mechanism uncovers more than just the foundations of human development and social connections. It reveals the core of our cravings for emotional stability and how our natural instincts shape our actions, weaving themselves into the tapestry of our surroundings. We're talking about the nitty-gritty of our primal selves and the powerful role they play in our lives.

Sure, you probably don't recall your attachment style from your diaper days, but there's a good chance you remember the vibes your caregiver gave off or how they made you feel when you were a kid. Those moments, whether warm and fuzzy or otherwise, stay with us and help create the emotional roadmap that guides us as adults.[10]

"Attachment researchers agree that, given the opportunity, all human infants become attached to their primary caregiver, typically within the first 8 months of life." [11]

PHASES OF ATTACHMENT

Now we know, attachment styles are shaped by various factors, including parental care and life experiences. By comprehending the impact of our upbringing and past relationships on our attachment style, we can create prototypes of different attachment styles. With this knowledge, we can form secure attachments with our loved ones.

Attachment theory proposes that there are four stages of attachment development:

1. **Pre-attachment phase (birth to 6 weeks):** While infants do not have a particular attachment to any one caregiver, they find solace in the presence of human contact.

2. **Attachment in the making (6 weeks to 6-8 months):** As infants mature, they tend to exhibit a preference for familiar caregivers and may experience distress when separated from them.

3. **Clear-cut attachment (6-8 months to 18-24 months):** As infants grow and develop, they tend to form stronger

attachments to specific caregivers and may display signs of separation anxiety when apart from them.

4. **Formation of reciprocal relationships (18-24 months and beyond):** As children grow, they tend to develop greater autonomy and establish more intricate connections with their caregivers that rely on mutual confidence and admiration.[12]

Attachment theory is kind of like a game of catch between a kid and their main cheerleader - mom, dad, or whoever's doing the heavy lifting. The ball zipping back and forth represents the bond between them. The kid's tosses (their actions and behaviors) can totally change how the cheerleader responds, and vice versa. If the cheerleader always catches the ball and tosses it back with a big smile (being sensitive to the kid's needs), it can help shape the kid's behavior and maybe even their personality.

When the kid feels like their cheerleader is always ready and willing to play catch, they develop a sense of security as solid as a well-worn mitt. This gives them the confidence to go explore the world, maybe even try out new games, because they know they've got a reliable "home base" to return to for a comforting pat on the back and a juice box. It's a win-win game![13]

 "A mother is not a person to lean on,
but a person to make leaning unnecessary."
– Dorothy Canfield Fisher

WHAT ALL THIS MEANS FOR EARLY ATTACHMENTS

Imagine children with **Anxious attachments** as little velcro sneakers. They constantly fret that their trusty laces (their parents) might come undone when they need them, turning them into mini worry-warts and making them stick closer than a stubborn burr.

These kiddos can also become as timid as a mouse in a cat convention, making them less eager to scamper off and explore the wide, wild world. But why the hesitation? Picture their parental care as an unpredictable roller coaster ride - sometimes it's a steady climb with supportive hands, but other times, it's a sudden drop with no one holding on.

It's also like when your favorite superhero show plays reruns instead of the new episode you were promised. Clinical research even suggests that using "time-out in the Fortress of Solitude" threats as a form of control might stick this "velcro" pattern on kids.[14]

Consider folks with **Avoidant** attachments as self-sufficient hermit crabs. They've learned to expect the chilly shoulder instead of a warm hug, more often than a polar bear expects snow. So they retreat into their shells and try to handle life's pinches on their own. They might even come across as more self-absorbed than a mirror later in life.

Why the shell game? Picture a little crab reaching out for a comforting claw, only to get a cold wave in return. If that happens enough, it's no wonder they decide to play it safe, stick to their shells, and adopt a crab's favorite motto: "I got this, no help needed.[15]

Then there are the **Disorganized** attachments. Disorganized attachment can happen when an infant is physically abused, neglected, or when a parent with bipolar disorder (or another personality disorder) treats their child unpredictably. Other causes are when a mother is preoccupied with mourning a lost parental figure from their childhood or if they suffered physical or sexual abuse as a child.[16]

 "One-year-olds' attachment patterns typically persist. This is because parent-child interactions frequently don't alter, and each pattern has the propensity to reinforce itself. Secure kids are pleasant and easier to handle, whereas anxious kids might be whining and avoidant youngsters may bully others. In both scenarios, the parent's response to the child's actions could result in a negative feedback loop." [17]

LATER IN CHILDHOOD

As kids grow up, their behavioral tendencies start to show. Around the age of six, you'll see children who have a secure attachment with their parents chatting away in a laid-back, friendly manner, enjoying open conversations. On the other hand, those with an anxious attachment style might display a mix of insecurity and frustration. Kids with an avoidant attachment style tend to opt for more formal, distant interactions, engaging in less personal chatter and often preferring to play solo.

In some cases, you might spot six-year-olds who seem disorganized or bewildered, trying to assert control over their parents, leading to disjointed conversations. These behavioral quirks are like little mirrors reflecting both the child's personality and the dynamics of their relationship with their parents.[18]

UNCONSCIOUS PATTERNS AKA "INTERNAL WORKING MODELS"

Attachment theory suggests that kids build behind-the-scenes mental models of themselves and the people they're attached to, like a secret roadmap for understanding and anticipating behavior, as well as orchestrating their responses. These internalized expectations morph into unspoken rules that direct attention, memory, and what they know about themselves, their attachment figures, and their relationships. While past relationships set the stage for these working models, it's the present relationships that can give them a makeover. The handoff of attachment from parents to children isn't a straight shot—it relies on the parent's working model, which influences their parenting style and ultimately, their little one's attachment.

Secure attachments lead to trust and fulfillment of needs, while insecure attachments result in negative internalizations and corresponding expectations. In secure attachments, children perceive their attachment figures as supportive and available, leading to beliefs that they are lovable. Securely attached children show competence and interest in exploring their environment and are skilled in social interactions. Two-thirds of middle-class infants tested are securely attached. Working models of attachment are stable and predictable, allowing for predictions of later relationship patterns based on early attachment quality, although intervening circumstances also shape later significant relationships.[19] Remember from up above, that all of our relationships are like a feedback loop. Together our experiences interlace to determine who we are and shape our responses. This is why it takes work to reprogram! Refocusing our energies on the "now" is where you and I are headed.

CHAPTER REVIEW

You may say, "Great, but how do I actually fix my relationships?" Knowing about your early attachment experiences and how your attachment style came to be is key. This understanding can help you tackle issues in your current attachments by shining a light on patterns in your relationships and nudging you towards self-reflection, ultimately setting the stage for healthier, more satisfying connections.

Recognizing the influence of your early attachment experiences on your present attachment style can help you become more conscious of your behavioral patterns and navigate them more effectively. Self-reflection also lends a hand in figuring out what you truly want and need in a relationship and whether your actions are just learned habits or honest desires.

In your Workbook you'll see some thoughtful exercises to assist with your self-reflection and a stronger understanding of your own childhood experiences.

Spend some time with those exercises now. Then, with those thoughts clear, we'll dive into the four attachment styles and start figuring out which one might be yours!

THE FOUR WAYS OF BEING IN RELATIONSHIPS

A Quartet Of Connections

Your attachment style is based not just on your own self-perception, but also on how you perceive others. Understanding this can be the key to unlocking healthier, more fulfilling relationships."

– Dr. Amir Levine and Rachel Heller

WELCOME TO THE CIRCUS

In the grand three-ring spectacle that is existence, we all assume the roles of emotional funambulists, perched atop the precarious high wire of our inner lives, reaching out with trembling hands to form connections with other aerialists. Welcome, my cherished audience, to the heart-thumping, head-scratching world of attachment styles—the unseen puppet strings that bind us to our fellow trapeze artists! In this daring, truth-defying expedition, we'll plunge headfirst into the psychological flying trapeze that flings us between love, loss, and the vast gray expanse in between. Buckle up those emotional seatbelts, as we're about to embark on a rollercoaster journey through the high-stakes carnival of human connection. Bid adieu to your emotional elephants, and prepare to tame the lions of your history as we conquer the art of attachment, one passionate somersault at a time. Together, we'll untangle the mysteries of our relational tightrope, and learn to cha-cha our way to a life of love and liberation. Welcome to the most dazzling spectacle on the planet: your emotional existence!

 "We must learn to reprogram our minds, comprehend our deepest pain points, mend the dynamics between ourselves and those close to us, and become aware of our subconscious mechanisms. In the subsequent chapters, we will offer valuable advice for achieving healing and personal growth."

We must also note that one attachment style in one relationship, or one experience if you will, can then impact how you behave in other relationships. So, while a lot of what has happened to us in our childhood is marked in our subconscious, continuous experiences also shape us as human beings are fluid people. What are your core beliefs? Know that these shift.

JO AND EMMA

The tales of attachment styles continue, dear readers. We've already met Avoidant Alex and Anxious Laura, but now it's time to explore the stories of Emma and Jo. Emma and Jo hail from vastly different universes, but their experiences have shaped their attachment styles in unique ways. Let's begin with Jo, shall we?

Jo's childhood was a world of wonder and whimsy. Her parents doted on her with endless love and support. Their abode was a haven of tranquility and stability, with steady routines and unconditional affection. Jo felt seen, heard, and secure in her family's warm embrace.

Jo's parents brought the essence of adventure into her life, taking her on fishing trips and embarking on other exciting expeditions. Through these shared experiences, Jo learned the importance of teamwork, patience, and quality time with loved ones. Her parents also demonstrated the art of healthy conflict resolution, never resorting to harsh words or belittling conduct. Instead, they resolved disputes with tenderness and constructive intent, teaching Jo the value of finding common ground while maintaining the bond of love and support. Jo felt free to express her emotions and needs candidly, and her parents validated her feelings, nurturing a sense of self-worth within her. This equilibrium enabled Jo to develop faith in her abilities while trusting that her parents would support her when needed.

In crafting this nurturing and supportive universe, Jo's parents laid the groundwork for her secure attachment style. They exemplified the pillars of open communication and emotional validation, which later served as a blueprint for Jo's relationships. Consequently, Jo stepped into adulthood equipped with the skills and emotional fortitude to forge deep, meaningful connections with others, spanning friendships and romantic partnerships alike.

Emma, on the other hand, had a much different experience. Her parents were inconsistent, emotionally distant, and often neglectful. Emma was left alone for long periods, and her parents' unpredictable behavior left her feeling anxious and scared. Her home life was chaotic, and she never knew what to expect.

In Emma's peculiar and disordered world, her parents unintentionally cultivated a disorganized attachment style through a myriad of experiences. For example, they would plan family excursions only to abruptly cancel them without reason or reschedule haphazardly. This inconsistency left Emma feeling insecure, as she could never be sure if her parents would honor their commitments.

Another distinct experience that shaped Emma's attachment style occurred when her parents left her with unfamiliar caregivers without warning. They would whisk her away to a neighbor's or a distant relative's home without bothering to introduce her or help her feel at ease in the new surroundings. This pattern of erratic care left Emma feeling forsaken and uncertain of who she could rely on.

Moreover, Emma's parents often quarreled in her presence without ever resolving the conflict or offering her solace. Witnessing this emotional chaos and unresolved strife left Emma feeling vulnerable and unsure of her place within her family. She would attempt to mediate, but her parents would either disregard her concerns or embroil her in their disagreements, further intensifying her feelings of instability and unease.

Compounding these challenges, Emma's parents neglected to provide her with emotional support or validation, frequently trivializing or disregarding her feelings. For instance, if Emma was distraught after a challenging day at school, her parents might dismiss her worries as inconsequential or unrelated, rendering her unheard and invalidated.

Emma's mother had always been critical of her appearance, but the comment she made during Emma's junior year of high school cut especially deep. Emma was sitting in the living room, engrossed in a book, when her mother walked in and asked to talk to her.

Emma put her book down and listened as her mother told her that she needed to consider getting a nose job. Her mother said that if Emma got a nose job, people would like her more and she would be more successful in life. Emma was shocked and hurt.

She tried to explain to her mother that she was happy with the way she looked and didn't want to change anything about herself. But her mother dismissed her concerns, telling her that she was being naive and that she needed to think about her future. She was always trying to maintain her balance while her mother pushed her towards an unhealthy, unrealistic standard of beauty. She began to count calories to gain what felt like a sense of control. She would obsessively run and exercise. Her mother encouraged this behavior even though it resulted in an eating disorder, that again, went dismissed by her parents.

Over the following months, Emma found herself scrutinizing her appearance, feeling like she was never good enough. She tried to talk to her mother about her feelings, but her mother continued to dismiss her concerns, telling her that she was overreacting. Emma felt like she was on an emotional tightrope, trying to navigate her way through her mother's criticism while staying true to herself.

These experiences contributed to Emma's disorganized attachment style, imbuing her with a sense of unpredictability, fear, and insecurity. The tumult and inconsistency of her home life hindered her ability to trust others, manage her emotions, and forge healthy relationships as she matured. Consequently, Emma grappled with establishing profound connections and maintaining stable, nurturing relationships in various facets of her life.

These early experiences shaped Jo and Emma's attachment styles. Jo developed a secure attachment style, meaning she had a healthy and positive attitude towards relationships. She was comfortable with intimacy, able to communicate her emotions, and trusted that others would be there for her. She had a strong sense of self-worth and was confident in her ability to navigate relationships.

Emma, on the other hand, developed a disorganized attachment style, meaning she struggled with fear, mistrust, and confusion in her relationships. She had trouble regulating her emotions, and her past experiences left her feeling unsure about how to approach intimacy. She often found herself pushing people away or clinging to them in unhealthy ways.

As they grew older, Jo and Emma's attachment styles began to impact their relationships. Jo had several long-term romantic relationships throughout her life. She found that she was able to communicate openly with her partners, set boundaries, and trust them. Her secure attachment style allowed her to form deep connections, and she felt happy and fulfilled in her relationships.

Emma, on the other hand, struggled to form healthy relationships. She often found herself attracted to people who were emotionally unavailable or who treated her poorly. She struggled to communicate her needs and often felt anxious and insecure in her relationships. She found herself constantly seeking validation from her partners, and when she didn't receive it, she would become even more anxious and needy.

One specific experience that demonstrated the impact of Emma's disorganized attachment style was her relationship with a man named Ryan. Ryan was charming, confident, and seemed to have everything together. Emma was initially drawn to him because she thought he could provide her with the stability and security she craved.

However, as their relationship progressed, Emma found herself becoming increasingly anxious and jealous. She would constantly check his social media accounts, interrogate him about his whereabouts, and accuse him of cheating. Ryan became increasingly frustrated with her behavior and began to distance himself.

Eventually, Emma's fears became a self-fulfilling prophecy. She discovered that Ryan had been seeing someone else behind her back, and the relationship ended in a messy and painful way. She had logged on to his computer while he was in the shower. Emma was devastated, and it took her a long time to recover from the experience. He immediately ended things, and asked her to leave. She dragged herself to the door in shame, unsure who was really in the wrong.

Jo, on the other hand, had a very different experience in her relationships. She had been dating a man named Mark for several years, and they had built a strong and healthy relationship based on mutual trust and respect. They communicated openly, shared their hopes and dreams with each other, and supported each other through difficult times.

An example of the strength of Jo's attachment style was when Mark lost his job. Jo was there for him every step of the way. She listened to him when he needed to vent, helped him with his job search, and reminded him that he was worthy and valuable regardless of his employment status.

Together, Jo and Mark weathered the storm, and their relationship grew even stronger as a result. They knew they could count on each other, and their love and commitment to each other only deepened over time.

In the end, Jo and Emma's attachment styles were shaped by their early childhood experiences, but they were not set in stone. With time, patience, and the right support, Emma could work through her disorganized attachment style and develop more healthy relationship patterns.

Emma sought therapy to address her attachment issues, and it proved to be a transformative experience. She learned to recognize her patterns of behavior and the underlying emotions that drove them. She also learned new strategies for coping with her anxiety and regulating her emotions. Over time, she began to feel more confident in her relationships and more secure in herself.

As a result, Emma began to attract healthier partners who treated her with respect and kindness. She learned to communicate her needs more effectively and set boundaries that protected her emotional well-being. Although it was not always easy, Emma found that the work she did on herself was well worth the effort.

In the end, Jo and Emma's attachment styles had a significant impact on their relationships. While Jo's secure attachment style allowed her to form deep and meaningful connections with others, Emma's disorganized attachment style made it challenging for her to trust and be vulnerable with others. Every text, or social event left her in bed for hours turning over interactions and implications of things people had said. What it meant, how did they view her? However, through hard work and self-reflection, Emma was able to overcome her attachment issues and develop more healthy relationship patterns. And in doing so, she discovered a new level of self-awareness and self-confidence that allowed her to thrive in all areas of her life.

THE SIDESHOW OF ATTACHMENT STYLES

First things first. We must remember through reading this book that a person (you) can have a dominant attachment style. Also! ...and sorry to confuse...it is possible you can have little bits of other attachment styles in varying situations. So it is not only important to read and learn about what you believe to be your main attachment style; it is equally important to learn about all four styles, and how to address them so that you can become the secure person you hope to be.

Secure Attachment Style

Individuals who sport a secure attachment style are akin to seasoned diplomats in the world of relationships. They have an uncanny knack for seeing the best in themselves and others - think rose-colored glasses, but the prescription is just right.

They're as comfortable with intimacy as a cat is with a sunbeam, and they can convey their needs and emotions with the finesse of a master linguist. Healthy boundaries for them are as natural as a well-tailored suit, and they're able to lend trust and support to their partners like a reliable old friend.

In the grand ballroom of adult relationships, these folks don't just waltz around the edges. No, they dive right in, forming deep and meaningful ties as effortlessly as a maestro conducts a symphony. For them, vulnerability isn't a chilling plunge into icy waters, but a soothing dip into a warm Jacuzzi under a starlit sky.

Avoidant Attachment Style

People sporting the avoidant attachment style could be likened to the elusive chameleons of the relationship jungle. They often view themselves and others through a somewhat gloomy lens - think of a cloudy day when you've forgotten your umbrella.

Intimacy for them can feel as comfortable as a pair of stilettos on a cobblestone street, leading them to dodge closeness in relationships like a master matador sidestepping a bull. Their communication style can sometimes resemble a cryptic crossword puzzle, making it a challenge to convey their needs and emotions.

Trust for them can be as hard to come by as a four-leaf clover in a field of three-leaf impostors. In the grand theater of adult relationships, these individuals may keep to the back row, preferring to keep their partners at arm's length or even eschew intimacy like a vampire avoids garlic. It's not that they don't want to join the performance, they're just a bit more cautious about forgetting their lines.

Anxious Attachment Style

People who've got that anxious attachment style on their psychological resumes tend to see themselves through a less-than-rosy lens, while painting others in a more flattering light – think self-portrait in charcoal, others in vibrant oils.
Their yearning for intimacy and closeness can be as strong as a caffeine-addict's need for that morning espresso, yet they might also feel as insecure as a penguin on a melting iceberg, constantly worrying about the chilly waters of rejection or abandonment.

They may be as sensitive to their partner's actions or emotions as a gourmet chef is to the hint of too much salt in the soup. Trust, for them, can be as slippery as a wet bar of soap in a tiled shower.

When it comes to the soap opera of adult relationships, these individuals might find themselves checking the 'ratings' a little too often, seeking a constant stream of reassurance from their co-star. In the sitcom of life, they're the ones always looking for a laugh track to confirm they're still part of the show.

Disorganized Attachment Style

Those navigating life with a disorganized attachment style could be likened to the eclectic playlist where opera collides with punk rock. Their early life experiences may have been as tumultuous as a stormy sea, leaving footprints of inconsistency in their attachment narratives. However, it's important to acknowledge that these individuals can also be gifted and creative in unique ways that stem from their ability to think outside the box.

Regulating their emotions and behaviors can be as challenging as herding cats, resulting in a relationship performance that could outdo the most dramatic telenovela. Their interactions can sometimes seem as unpredictable as a jack-in-the-box, leaving those around them guessing. Yet, in their chaos, disorganized individuals can also bring an element of surprise and spontaneity to relationships that can be exciting and invigorating.

These individuals might find themselves weaving threads of trust, intimacy, and communication with the tentative hands of a beginner. They may occasionally pick up the scissors of self-sabotage, snipping the threads they've just woven, not out of malice, but more likely due to a blurry blueprint. However, with time and self-reflection, those with a disorganized attachment style can develop a better understanding of their own patterns and behaviors, learning to harness their creativity and unique perspective to build stronger, healthier relationships.

 "Creative minds are rarely tidy."
– John William Gardner

It's important to note that attachment styles can be fluid and can change over time, particularly with therapy and self-reflection. We can also have a bit of one attachment style in certain relationships, and another in a different scenario. However, recognizing one's own attachment style and understanding how it can impact adult relationships can be a valuable tool in developing healthier relationship patterns.

ATTACHMENT STYLES AND YOUR RELATIONSHIPS

The Balancing Act of Relationships

Secure Attachment Style

Individuals with a secure attachment style possess a unique gift, a gift that allows them to glide through the often choppy waters of relationships with an ease and grace that eludes so many of us. These individuals know how to forge deep and meaningful connections with their friends, family, and romantic partners, striking the perfect balance between trust and vulnerability, and respecting boundaries with a quiet and unassuming confidence. In their friendships, they create an atmosphere of trust and openness, a safe haven where their friends feel seen, heard, and valued. Within their families, they communicate with honesty, empathy, and mutual respect, weaving a tapestry of connection that is strong and enduring. And in matters of the heart, they know how to create a bond that is both profound and sustainable, responding to the needs of their partners with tenderness and care, while honoring the need for independence and autonomy. Truly, these individuals possess a gift that is both rare and precious, a gift that allows them to create and sustain relationships that are healthy, fulfilling, and full of joy.

Avoidant Attachment Style

When it comes to forming deep and meaningful relationships, those with an avoidant attachment style might have a bit of a tough time. They can come off as emotionally distant or guarded, making it tricky for others to get close in platonic relationships. And in family dynamics, they might avoid emotional conversations or keep interactions at a minimum. When it comes to romantic relationships, those with an avoidant attachment style may struggle with committing, expressing their emotions, or relying on their partner. As a result, their relationships may be fleeting or lack emotional depth. But hey, let's not judge too harshly - we all have our own unique styles when it comes to relating to others.

Anxious Attachment Style

For those with an anxious attachment style, relationships can pose a number of challenges. In platonic friendships, they may find themselves constantly seeking reassurance from their friends, creating an impression of neediness or clinginess that can strain the relationship and potentially drive friends away. Within familial relationships, their heightened sensitivity to criticism or rejection can complicate the establishment of healthy boundaries and hinder open communication. And when it comes to romantic relationships, those with an anxious attachment style may become fixated on their partner, seeking constant validation and fearing abandonment. This fixation can manifest as jealousy, controlling behaviors, or an unhealthy reliance on their partner for emotional support. Clearly, an anxious attachment style can pose significant obstacles when it comes to building and maintaining healthy relationships, but with time, patience, and perhaps some guidance, these individuals can learn to navigate their relationships with greater ease and confidence.

Disorganized Attachment Style

Disorganized attachment styles can generate instability and confusion in adult relationships. In platonic friendships, individuals with a disorganized attachment style may struggle to form and maintain stable, enduring friendships due to their capricious behavior and trust issues. Familial relationships might be marked by strained communication, emotional distance, and erratic or inconsistent conduct. In romantic relationships, individuals with a disorganized attachment style may find it difficult to form secure attachments, frequently displaying a push-pull dynamic with their partner. They may struggle to effectively communicate their needs or engage in self-sabotaging behavior, making it challenging to cultivate and maintain a healthy, long-term relationship.

THE VAST WORLD AROUND US

In the mysterious depths of human connection, we unearth the intricate layers of attachment, each with its own unique narrative. Like the roots of an ancient tree, intertwining and reaching out, our relationships are shaped by the diverse attachment styles that we bring into them. Secure, anxious, avoidant, and disorganized – these are the threads that weave our relational tapestry. We must seek to understand their prevalence, variations across cultures and contexts, and most importantly, why they're worth paying attention to.

In the vast ocean of humanity, approximately 60% of individuals sail the seas of life with a secure attachment style. Anchored in their own worthiness and the reliability of others, these individuals embody the essence of stable and nurturing connections. Like a steady lighthouse guiding a ship through stormy waters, their relationships provide a safe haven where vulnerability and trust coexist.

As we journey through the spectrum of attachment, we encounter the anxious attachment style, prevalent in roughly 5.5% of the population. These individuals, caught in the tempest of emotional turmoil, cling to their partners with intense fervor, fearing abandonment and seeking constant reassurance. The anxious heart yearns for connection, but the very intensity of this yearning can repel others.

On the opposite side of the spectrum lies the avoidant attachment style, characterizing around 22% of individuals. Like a leaf adrift on a breeze, these souls float through life, shunning closeness and steering clear of emotional entanglements. They construct barriers around their hearts, often appearing aloof and self-sufficient, even as they secretly long for connection.

Lastly, we find the disorganized attachment style, present in a smaller percentage of the population, around 8%. These individuals are ensnared in a labyrinth of conflicting emotions, vacillating between the need for closeness and the fear of it. Their relationships are a complex dance of approach and avoidance, as they grapple to find balance and stability.[20,21]

CONCLUSION

The prevalence of these attachment styles is not set in stone, for the landscape of human connection is ever-evolving. It's important to recognize that culture and context play a significant role in shaping our attachment patterns. In collectivist societies, where interdependence and communal bonds are valued, one might expect higher rates of secure attachment, as individuals learn to rely on and trust one another. Conversely, in individualistic cultures that prize self-reliance and autonomy, the prevalence of avoidant attachment may be more pronounced.

As we examine these attachment styles, we are reminded of the oceans of human relationships. Understanding the prevalence and variation of attachment styles across cultures offers us valuable insights into the nature of our connections with others. By paying attention to these styles, we give ourselves the opportunity to cultivate deeper, more nurturing relationships – for it is through such connections that we truly come alive.

In the end, our attachment styles are like roots that intertwine and interact to create the complex network that is our emotional life. By shining a light on these patterns, we are not only acknowledging their existence, but we are also inviting ourselves to grow, to heal, and to love more fully. So, let us pay attention to these relational threads, for they have the power to transform our relationships and our very selves. We will see next in Chapter four just how the magic of a secure attachment style can create a beautiful liife of fulfilment.[22]

4

SECURE:
THE FOUNDATION OF
HEALTHY RELATIONSHIPS

In the Windy City, where skyscrapers kiss the clouds and the scent of deep-dish pizza wafts through the air, Eduardo strolled the streets as a 30-year-old man who could seemingly charm the stars from the sky. His ability to forge connections with people from all walks of life was uncanny, to say the least. Eduardo"s well-kept secret? He had, unknowingly, a secure attachment style.

To understand Eduardo's attachment style, one must delve into the depths of his childhood, where his doting parents, Ellen and George, cultivated an atmosphere of warmth and support. They were staunch advocates of trust and security within their familial enclave, and Eduardo reaped the benefits of this upbringing. Aided by their unwavering emotional support and guidance, Eduardo's confidence blossomed like a peony in springtime.

Open communication was the lifeblood of the family, and young Eduardo was encouraged to vocalize his feelings and thoughts with unbridled candor. This expressive skill set proved invaluable in his later years, forming the bedrock of his secure attachment style.

Eduardo's love life was as fascinating as the winding corridors of the Art Institute of Chicago. Enter Layla, his charming and equally secure-attachment-styled girlfriend. Together, they navigated the peaks and valleys of their relationship with the grace of figure skaters gliding across the ice at Millennium Park. Communication was their North Star, guiding them through the most turbulent of times and fostering a sense of safety and trust.

Their conversations delved into the deepest recesses of their souls, as they recounted past experiences and reflected on how these shaped their present selves. It was through these intimate exchanges that Eduardo gained insight into his attachment style, recognizing the importance of working through any lingering attachment-related issues.

Eduardo's friends, an eclectic mix of personalities, found solace in his steadfast presence. He was the glue that bound them together, the epitome of reliability, offering his unwavering support at every turn. It was not uncommon for Eduardo to be the first port of call when the storms of life raged, his friends seeking his counsel and comforting embrace.

In his pursuit of fostering secure attachments, once he realized he could be a pillar for others, Eduardo dedicated time to practice emotional regulation and communication skills. He attended workshops and sought the guidance of a skilled therapist, unraveling the complexities of his inner world. This quest for self-improvement not only strengthened his relationships but also equipped him with the tools necessary for weathering the emotional storms that inevitably arise in life.

Eduardo''s social calendar brimmed with activities that promoted positive social interactions and connections. From impromptu picnics at the shores of Lake Michigan to spirited games of beach volleyball, Eduardo reveled in the camaraderie and laughter that permeated his life. He was a firm believer in the power of shared experiences, understanding that these moments were the building blocks of strong and lasting friendships.

As the years progressed, Eduardo's secure attachment style became an indelible part of his identity, much like the iconic Cloud Gate sculpture nestled in the heart of Chicago. It was this attachment style that laid the foundation for his remarkable ability to connect with others, an ability that left a lasting impression on those who crossed his path.

The story of Eduardo, the charming man from Chicago with the secure attachment style, serves as a testament to the power of nurturing relationships, fostering trust, and engaging in self-reflection. It is a shining example of how one man's journey of personal growth can ripple outward, touching the lives of those around him and creating a world of meaningful connections that span a lifetime.

SECURE, WITH BENEFITS

In the labyrinth of human connection, one encounters the glimmering gem of secure attachment, a treasure trove of benefits that elevates relationships to new heights. Those fortunate enough to possess this attachment style find their romantic bonds richer, their hearts lighter, as they navigate the complexities of love with a sense of ease and understanding.

On this dance floor of romance, secure attachment waltzes its way to the forefront, encouraging an open exchange of thoughts and emotions that seals connection between partners. This attachment style acts as a beacon, guiding lovers to the shores of greater relationship satisfaction, where intimacy and closeness are celebrated and cherished.

Communication becomes the lifeblood of these secure attachments, flowing effortlessly through the veins of their relationships, allowing for a dialogue that is candid and free of fear. Words dance gracefully between partners, bridging gaps and forging a connection that is nothing short of extraordinary.

At the heart of this connection lies the promise of emotional intimacy, the jewel in the crown of secure attachment's myriad gifts. Lovers, emboldened by their trust, delve into the depths of each other's souls, discovering a sanctuary where love blossoms and thrives in its purest form. This profound intimacy becomes a refuge, a haven where hearts unite and find solace in one another.

Beyond the realm of romantic love, secure attachment shines its light in other facets of life. Empathy blooms, nourished by a heightened ability to distinguish between the self and others, influenced by both interpersonal and contextual factors. Secure attachment also offers a shield against paranoia, negative emotions, and cognitive entanglement, while fostering positivity and encouraging help-seeking behaviors.

In professional settings, secure attachment reveals itself as a valuable ally. Those who embody this attachment style are often perceived by supervisors as more proficient in their tasks, adept at balancing autonomy and collaboration as required.

In essence, secure attachment bestows upon those who embrace it a wealth of gifts that transcend the boundaries of love and life. It is the golden ability for connection, an invaluable asset that serves as a compass, guiding individuals towards richer, more fulfilling relationships and experiences.[23,24]

THANKS, MOM!

In the beginning, when the world is still a formless void, early childhood experiences define the very core of attachment style development. The presence of caregivers, responsive and nurturing, become essential as they bestow upon the child a secure base, from which they can venture into the world and forge a sense of trust and safety.

In the wild world of childhood, kids who luck out with caregivers who consistently have their backs are more likely to develop that oh-so-desirable secure attachment style. It's like winning the emotional lottery, complete with a positive view of self and others and a rock-solid belief that their needs will be met. But then there are the kids who get stuck with less-than-stellar caregiving – they're the ones tiptoeing on the tightrope of insecure attachment, often struggling to build and maintain relationships for the long haul.

But don't despair, because research has shown that it's totally possible to go from insecure to secure attachment styles, proving that humans are nothing if not resilient. So, whether you're a kid or a grown-up, nurturing and supportive relationships are the key to unlocking your potential for change and growth. Hang in there – it's never too late to turn things around.[25]

1+1 = ?

You'd think that when it comes to choosing a partner, we'd naturally gravitate towards someone with a similar attachment style, right? But prior research on dating and married couples has shown that's not always the case. Apparently, even though secure individuals tend to prefer secure partners, it's not a guarantee.

I mean, it makes sense. We're all complicated beings with unique experiences and perspectives. So it's not surprising that we might be drawn to someone who's a little different from us, even in terms of attachment style.

But what does it all mean? Well, it suggests that we have the capacity to work through differences in our attachment styles, even if it takes a little more effort. And who knows, maybe learning to navigate those differences can even strengthen our relationships in the long run.[26]

According to one study that's in the business of attachment styles and couple relationships, it turns out that people with a secure attachment style are way more likely to engage in positive and less drama-filled behaviors in their relationships[27]. Another study found that having a secure attachment style means you're less likely to engage in risky sexual behavior.[28]

A recent study on dating couples has unearthed some intriguing findings. Dual-secure couples, for instance, have been found to experience less suppression of their negative feelings compared to dual-insecure couples. Moreover, these secure couples are less likely to perceive their partners as suppressing their negative emotions. The study offers an illuminating glimpse into the dynamics of romantic relationships and how attachment styles can influence emotional regulation.[29]

It's explained that a securely attached person is someone who has internalized a reliable relationship with their caregivers during infancy. This early connection allows them to navigate different social situations with ease and maintain a healthy balance between self-regulation and interpersonal regulation of stress. They're adaptable to various social contexts and show remarkable resilience when faced with traumatic stress.[30]

So, in a nutshell, people with a secure attachment style generally have a pretty positive view of themselves and others, are all about that intimacy, and can communicate their needs and emotions like champions.

SOME PRACTICAL ADVICE

If you're looking to develop secure attachments (and let's be honest, who isn't?), I've got some practical advice for you that's as helpful as a pocket on a shirt:

1. First things first, surround yourself with nurturing relationships involving mentors, friends, and, you know, the kind of people who make you feel like they've got your back and are rooting for you.[31,32]

2. Work on fostering that warm and fuzzy sense of safety and trust in your relationships. The goal here is to create an environment where everyone feels secure enough to share their deepest thoughts, dreams, and Netflix passwords.

3. Take a little stroll down memory lane and reflect on past experiences. If you find any attachment-related issues lurking in the shadows, consider chatting with a therapist or counselor. They're like emotional Sherpas, guiding you through the rough terrain of your feelings.

4. Practice makes perfect, so give emotional regulation and communication skills a whirl. Think of it as flexing your emotional muscles – the more you work out, the stronger you become.

5. Finally, engage in activities that promote positive social interactions and connections. It's like the saying goes: "The more, the merrier." So, go out and find your merry little tribe.[33]

If you are reading this and thinking to yourself, hmm, it sounds like my attachment style doesn't necessarily measure up to being secure; don't worry. You can heal your way there.

HEALING TECHNIQUE

You know what they call it when you go back and forth between feeling tense or uncomfortable in your body and then focusing on more neutral or pleasant sensations? Pendulation. Most learn about it during Somatic Experiencing therapy, which is all about healing trauma and stress-related disorders.

Basically, my therapist guided me through this process where I'd notice where I was feeling tight or sore, and then I'd shift my focus to a spot where I felt more at ease. Like a pendulum swinging back and forth, you know? It's all about building awareness of both the discomfort and the pleasure that our bodies can experience.

Step 1: Setup Shop

Find a spot that's as peaceful as a Zen master meditating on a mountaintop. Whether you're sprawling on a plush rug or curled up on your favorite armchair, get yourself nice and comfy. You can shut your peepers if you fancy. This is all about you, after all.

Step 2: Body Inspection

Once you're settled, it's time to play detective! Start by taking a few leisurely breaths. As you do, make a mental note of the sensations in your body. Got a tight spot? A sore muscle? Just observe these sensations like a non-judgmental, tea-sipping Sherlock Holmes. No need to change a thing.

Step 3: Shifty Business

Now for a bit of a switcheroo. Move your attention to a part of your body where you feel as relaxed as a cat snoozing in the sunshine. Could be your hands, feet, or even your nose - who am I to judge? Spend a few moments just basking in this comfort, like you're lounging on a tropical beach.

Step 4: The Pendulum Game

Ready for a bit of fun? Picture a pendulum swinging. Now, imagine your awareness is that pendulum. Swing it from the discomfort in your body to the comfort. Do this a few times, and voila! You're building resilience and acceptance faster than a barista whips up a latte.

Step 5: Mental Gymnastics

Who said gymnastics was all flips and tumbles? This step is all about flexing your mental muscles. Bring your focus to an upsetting, angry, or sad thought. Don't shy away from it, but don't get lost in it either.

Next, flip to a happier channel. Think of something pleasant, hopeful, or blissful. Spend some time here, just like you're enjoying a favorite book.

Just like before, start swinging your awareness between these thoughts. It's not just about being happy, it's about accepting all thoughts and feelings.

Step 6: The Home Stretch

Now, gently return your attention back to your surroundings. Draw in a few more deep breaths, like you're savoring the last bites of a delicious meal. When you're ready, open your eyes (if they were closed). You've completed the journey!

Remember, this isn't about escaping the bad or clinging to the good. It's about understanding the ebb and flow, the highs and lows. It's about developing a balanced relationship with your mind and body.

Of course, if you're new to this, it's always helpful to have a guide - a therapist, a mentor, or a trained professional. After all, even Frodo had Gandalf!

And let me tell you, it's not easy. But my therapist would gently nudge me to explore these sensations, encouraging me to lean into the relaxation and pleasure. It's like retraining your nervous system to regulate itself and release all that stored tension.

I'm a believer. I think pendulation is one of the most effective techniques out there for getting in touch with your body, mind, and finding a sense of balance. The cool part is you can practice this literally, anywhere, anytime!

Workbook: Take note of how this practice makes you feel, write the associations and connections you make.

CONCLUSION

In the quiet spaces between moments, Eduardo's story emerges as a testament to the significance of secure attachment styles in cultivating relationships that nourish and enrich our lives. Born from a childhood cocoon of support and tenderness, secure attachment gifts individuals with the ability to foster trust, communicate effectively, and weave connections that hold meaning. Although secure souls might not always find their counterparts, they possess the strength to traverse differences and fortify their bonds.

The formation of a secure attachment style demands immersing oneself in relationships that nourish, constructing havens where emotions flow freely, contemplating past experiences, honing emotional regulation and communication skills, and engaging in activities that foster positive connections. Pendulation, the subtle dance between discomfort and ease, whether in sensations or thoughts, can serve as a potent instrument for healing and seeking equilibrium.

Embracing secure attachment bestows a bounty of benefits upon both romantic and professional spheres of life, nurturing empathy, resilience, and emotional intimacy. By fostering secure attachments, individuals possess the power to transform their own existence and craft enduring, meaningful connections that resonate within the hearts of those they touch.

Not everyone has a secure attachment, and that's ok. In our next chapter, Chapter 5, we will begin to see how attachment styles can ebb toward the avoidant, and how these patterns can be addressed.

THE COMPLICATED WORLD OF AVOIDANT ATTACHMENT

The Art Of Distance

Avoidant attachment is like a long, lonely road—seemingly safe and predictable, but often leaving one yearning for the warmth of a nearby soul.

– Dr. Diane Poole Heller

In the stillness of their being, those with avoidant attachment styles seem to retreat into themselves, embracing an almost fierce independence, shrouded in emotional distance, and seldom allowing the warmth of intimacy to breach their lives. They become overburdened when depended upon too heavily. Deep within their subconscious, core beliefs whisper a narrative of unworthiness, perpetuating a sense of defectiveness. Within the quiet corners of their mind, thoughts of being defective may manifest in various forms, haunting and pervasive. They might experience thoughts such as:

"I am not good enough, and I will never be."

"Others are bound to discover my flaws, so it's better to keep my distance."

"I don't deserve happiness or success because of my imperfections."

"If someone gets to know the real me, they will inevitably be disappointed."

"My mistakes define me, and I can't escape them."

"I am unlovable, and people will eventually abandon me."

"I must constantly prove my worth, or others will see me as a failure."

"It's safer to avoid getting too close to others, for my flaws might hurt them too."

"I should not burden others with my problems; I must deal with them on my own."

"I am broken, and there is no hope for me to change or heal."

Do any of these thoughts relate to your own? These thoughts, often repetitive and intrusive, cast a shadow over the individual's sense of self and their ability to forge meaningful connections with others. They come to understand that vulnerability is a harbinger of pain and that the world of others is unsafe.

Grown-ups who embody the dismissive/avoidant attachment style often appear content with their own identity and situation. They may be sociable, laid-back, and a delight to spend time with. Moreover, these folks typically enjoy an ample circle of friends and, perhaps, numerous romantic liaisons. By and large, they're neither lonesome nor isolated outwardly. But their internal world could feel lonesome while surrounded by everyone who loves them; a silo of despair.

Avoidant adults, once children abandoned or neglected, learned to find solace in their own company, mastering the art of self-soothing, and depending solely on themselves. They traverse the landscape of life, a quiet testament to self-reliance, yet ever so cautiously, in case vulnerability betrays them once more.[34] Please remember this can change over time. We will address ways to do this at the end of this chapter.

Avoidant adults have a penchant for self-reliance. They possess robust self-esteem and don't lean on others for validation or emotional sustenance. These individuals often prioritize their professional growth, drawing confidence from each personal triumph. It's as if they've got everything under control.[35]

Hazan and Shaver (1987) first proposed the idea that the emotional connections seen in grown-up romances might resemble the bonds between little ones and their main caretakers. They believed that grown-up love connections could be sorted into the trio of categories created by Ainsworth and her team. Significantly, folks with avoidant tendencies experienced romantic relationships tinged with a hesitancy about closeness and a general unease around true intimacy.[36]

Curiously enough, the landscape of human attachment often displays ambivalent individuals steering clear of similar partners, while avoidant individuals do the same. In instances where the woman is ambivalent and the man is avoidant, such relationships persist, though they leave participants less than fulfilled. Attachment scholars posit that these ambivalent-avoidant unions arise from a social selection process in which individuals gravitate toward partners whose behavior aligns with their own expectations, or "working models," of relationships. When an ambivalent person encounters an avoidant partner who resists intimacy and closeness, their preexisting assumptions about relationships—namely, that others are hesitant to grow close and unwilling to commit—are reinforced.[37]

FRIENDSHIP WITH AN AVOIDANT

In the realm of avoidant attachments, one finds that social bonds and encounters linger on the surface. A profound depth is required for relationships to be truly gratifying and significant. Yet, when confronted with avoidant attachment styles, one may stumble upon an invisible wall.

These individuals permit others to dwell in their proximity, yet they maintain a certain distance. Evading the intensity of emotion and intimacy, they shield themselves from the vulnerability of closeness. As relationships venture into deeper waters, the dismissive/avoidant souls retreat within themselves. They may end relationships abruptly.

Amidst this emotional impasse, they might search for justifications to dismantle the bond. Easily exasperated by their partner's habits, behaviors, or appearance, they commence a gradual withdrawal. Entrenched in their belief, they declare emotional intimacy to be unnecessary.

The roots of this conviction lie within their childhood. Caregivers, unable or unwilling to offer support, have instilled in them a sense of mistrust. Once seeking solace and understanding, they found only disappointment. Consequently, they abandon the pursuit of emotional connection, as if extinguishing an inner flame.[38]

ROMANCE WITH AN AVOIDANT

Thais Gibson's *Attachment Theory: A Guide for Strengthening the Relationships in Your Life* offers valuable insights into how avoidant attachment can create challenges in forming and maintaining intimate relationships. This attachment style's impact on mental health and well-being can be profound, as it shapes an individual's ability to connect with others.

Avoidant attachment, as described by Gibson, often stems from early experiences where caregivers failed to provide adequate emotional support, leading to a deep-rooted belief that emotional intimacy is not essential. As a result, individuals with this attachment style tend to maintain emotional distance in relationships, believing that self-reliance is the key to happiness.

This emotional distancing can make it difficult for avoidant individuals to form deep, meaningful connections with others. Especially in love. They may struggle to open up and share their feelings, which can hinder the development of trust and intimacy in relationships. In turn, this can create a cycle of self-sabotage, as their reluctance to engage emotionally may push potential partners away.

The impact of avoidant attachment on mental health and well-being is also significant. Gibson highlights that the lack of emotional intimacy can contribute to feelings of loneliness and isolation, even when avoidant individuals are surrounded by people who care for them. This can lead to an increased risk of developing anxiety, depression, and other mental health challenges.

Additionally, the constant suppression of emotions can take a toll on an individual's overall well-being. Avoidant individuals may struggle to develop effective coping strategies for dealing with stress, as they are not accustomed to seeking support from others. They would rather let relationships fall to the wayside than ask for help. This can further exacerbate their mental health issues and contribute to a lower quality of life. It can even impact physical health as stress tends to do.

THE WORKPLACE AND THE AVOIDANT

Let's not forget that each attachment style has its own merits! Interestingly, there are unique strengths of dismissive avoidant employees within a professional environment.

Workers who exhibit dismissive avoidant attachment can be seen as selfless team players, as they often experience personal unease while enriching the lives of their coworkers. A study conducted by Ein-Dor and colleagues (2010) demonstrated that although insecure attachment styles can have detrimental effects on individuals, they may also offer evolutionary benefits.

This intriguing paradox is clarified by the notion that despite the personal disadvantages of possessing insecure attachments, there are substantial collective gains. Consequently, the presence of insecure attachment styles might not be accidental but rather, a product of evolutionary processes.

Employees with avoidant attachment styles have the capacity to boost their team's efficiency and preserve resources. These individuals are recognized for their swift reactions to threats, which proves advantageous in a work environment as they can quickly identify issues and allocate sufficient time to resolve them or minimize their impact.

These individuals tend to be self-reliant and rarely seek the support of others when making decisions. Their independence and confidence in their professional capabilities often lead to increased efficiency and reduced resource demand in the workplace.

When facing tight deadlines, avoidant employees are often the ones who get the job done. Since they are less focused on socializing at work, they are more likely to concentrate their efforts on their tasks and performance.

Individuals with avoidant attachment styles are inclined to push themselves towards success and excellence in their careers. As they are less concerned with fostering personal relationships, they devote themselves to their jobs and professional development. Consequently, avoidant individuals often rise to the top.[39]

HEALING ADVICE: PROBLEM SOLVING

When it comes to the aims of interpersonal effectiveness skills, the sage advice of Dr. Marsha Linehan comes to mind. Her first objective revolves around enhancing your ability to articulate your wants and needs, persuading others to take on tasks, compelling others to consider your views, and deftly saying "no" to unwanted requests. Essentially, these skills are about fostering assertiveness and clarity in your communications, enabling you to navigate social landscapes with greater ease.

Beyond individual interactions, these skills also extend to the realm of relationship management. They involve strengthening existing bonds, preventing the build-up of resentment, and mending relationships when needed. They empower you to address conflicts before they escalate and help in forging new connections. Moreover, they guide you in recognizing when a relationship has no room for improvement and needs to be ended. The final goal is striking a balance, a middle path, within relationships. This involves maintaining equilibrium and harmonizing acceptance with the drive for positive transformation. By mastering these skills, you can cultivate healthier, more fulfilling relationships that contribute positively to your life.

When a problem presents itself, as they tend to do in life, we have options. According to Marsha M. Linehan's DBT skills and training book these are some options people usually opt for, some of them are less constructive than others, for example, staying mad.[40]

1. Solve the problem using interpersonal effectiveness skills, walk the middle path, use problem solving skills. (emotional regulation skills)

2. Change feelings about the problem; using emotional regulation skills.

3. Accept the problem; use distress tolerance and mindfulness skills

4. Stay mad

Linehan suggests something called chain analysis which basically leads you to understanding your behaviors.

Below are some helpful ways to do this and you'll find this list repeated and expanded in your Workbook with space for your comments and discoveries.

- Identify triggers: Recognize situations, events, or emotions that prompt avoidant attachment behaviors.

- Observe responses: Take note of the immediate emotional and physical reactions to the triggers.

- Assess coping mechanisms: Analyze the strategies employed to distance oneself from emotions or relationships.

- Examine consequences: Evaluate the short-term and long-term effects of avoidant behaviors on relationships and personal well-being.

- Explore alternative responses: Consider healthier ways to address emotions and maintain connections with others.

- Implement change: Gradually replace avoidant behaviors with more adaptive and constructive responses.

- Monitor progress: Continuously assess improvement and adjust strategies as needed to foster secure attachments.

If you recognize now by reading this chapter that you or someone you love may have an avoidant personality, it could be possible that you would benefit from the above- mentioned "interpersonal effectiveness" skills.

CONCLUSION

Avoidant attachment styles often stem from a lack of emotional support during childhood, leading individuals to maintain emotional distance in relationships and prioritize self-reliance. This style can create challenges in forming and maintaining intimate connections, but it also has unique strengths in professional settings, such as boosting team efficiency and resource preservation. Healing and improving interpersonal skills can be achieved through methods like Dialectical Behavior Therapy (DBT), which helps individuals recognize triggers, evaluate coping mechanisms, and implement healthier responses. Developing these skills can enhance relationships, personal well-being, and overall quality of life. These skills take practice, in everyday life, so utilize your Workbook and practice in social situations. Every. Single. Day!

Chapter six will now seem paradoxical to all that you've gleaned. On the opposite end of the spectrum, anxious attachment is anything but avoidant. And that's ok.

6

NAVIGATING INTIMACY WITH ANXIOUS ATTACHMENT

Echoes Of Longing

Anxious attachment might feel like an emotional rollercoaster, oscillating between fear and relief. But it's also a testament to the strength of one's capacity for passion and commitment.

– Dr. Sue Johnson

GROWTH

Clara, a girl from Long Island, was born into the trappings of wealth and privilege, swaddled in the silken threads of her family's fortune. Yet beneath this veneer of opulence, she harbored an anxious attachment style that left her hungry for the love and attention of those around her. Her neediness and jealousy were insatiable, and she craved constant affirmation from her social circle like a parched desert flower thirsting for rain.

To the world, Clara appeared to have it all - beauty, wealth, and charm. But in truth, she was a solitary figure, friendless and unloved. She was a moth to the flame of human connection, seeking the warmth of their gaze and the light of their admiration. But the flame, ever elusive, continued to dance just beyond her reach. She once invited friends over to her beach house to swim but they all just wanted to marvel at her wealth and snicker at the obscenity of her life. She sensed all of this and threw a fit, screaming at a girl who she had been envious of for a very long time; Layla. Layla got along with others easily. She was an oddball and Clara couldn't quite figure her out, or win over her friendship. The quarrel ended with Layla throwing Clara's Miu Miu purse into the pool as everyone laughed.

Clara, determined to win the adoration she so desperately sought, delved into the art world, a realm where she could demonstrate her intellect and sophistication. In the art world if you aren't a true freak, you have to buy your way in. She was no mere ornament, no mere pretty face to be admired and then forgotten. Clara was a woman of substance, of depth, and she would prove it to them all.

With her father's wealth as her anchor, she established an art gallery of her own - a showcase for her keen eye and discerning taste, which was undoubtedly pristine. The kind of eye that you cannot buy. She knew this about herself. The gallery flourished, and soon, her name was whispered among the elite and the cultured. It was not enough to bask in the glow of her newfound success, however; Clara desired the respect and appreciation of her peers, and she would stop at nothing to obtain it. Whispers and conversations circulate about the art that was shown at her gallery. Was it conceptual enough? Did it merely reflect a surface taste, curated like that of an instagram grid? It didn't matter. People talking was enough to elicit conversations from the entire scene; lowbrow, hightbrow, fashionistas, B-list celebs, and downtown podcasters.

But beneath the sheen of her accomplishments lay Clara's core wounds, the scars that shaped her heart and mind. She had been raised by a mother who was beautiful but cold, a glittering icicle that never thawed. The warmth and love Clara so desperately craved were denied to her, leaving her with an insatiable hunger for affection.

Her father, a self-made tycoon, lavished her with material gifts but was absent in spirit, his heart buried beneath the weight of his fortune. He knew the price of everything but the value of nothing, least of all his daughter's love. His shame reflected back onto her. She carried his burden without even knowing it. Subconsciously, she knew exactly where she stood in the world. This obsessive thinking made her immensely sensitive to her surroundings. It was a sort of gift in its own right. Yet, It was this environment that had molded Clara into the woman she had become - desperate, lonely, and forever seeking approval.

As Clara continued her ascent in the art world, she slowly began to recognize the depths of her wounds. It was not the admiration of strangers she longed for but the love of those who had been meant to nurture her. She yearned to feel the warmth of her mother's embrace, the pride in her father's eyes. But these were specters that haunted her dreams, ghosts that would never be.

In the end, Clara's journey through the world of art and her unquenchable thirst for validation became a mirror, reflecting back her own fractured self. It was a portrait of a girl longing to be seen and loved, an image that could not be mended by the brushstrokes of success or the adoration of strangers. And yet, Clara found solace and, perhaps, the first glimmers of self-love.

THE ANXIOUS ONE

A fretful attachment style, a weight often hoisted upon the young, arises from the uneven choreography of parenting. At times, parents seem attuned and receptive to their offspring's needs, only to be discordant in the next breath. This confusion casts a veil of doubt over the child's bond with their caregivers, leaving them eternally pondering what lies ahead.

This attachment style is further tangled by the caregivers' "emotional starvation." In such cases, caregivers yearn for emotional or physical closeness with their children not to meet the child's needs, but to appease their own cravings. They may appear invasive or excessively vigilant, using the child to satisfy their own longing for affection or to uphold a specific façade, such as exemplifying the perfect parent. Yet, they do not genuinely invest the time required to forge a real connection with the child.

The kind of connection that neither a ski trip to Vail nor a two-week catamaran getaway with a private chef can purchase. Quality holds significance, but it should not be romanticized. Experiencing life in unison, through the thick and thin, is what ultimately weaves robust ties and enduring memories.

At the core of a child's maturation, the existence of a steadfast and reliable caregiver is indispensable. But for those burdened with anxious attachment, they carry the marks of never quite feeling sufficient, perpetually anticipating rejection. Their parents may have offered their love, only to withdraw it, akin to a haunting refrain echoing in perpetuity.

Sometimes, the inconsistency stems from parents who mean well, but find themselves stretched thin, caught in the whirlwind of work and travel, and the general demands of capitalism. These parents carry within them the ability to connect with their child, but time and distance often steal away the opportunity.

In a world where young hearts crave consistency, the ebb and flow of affection leave an indelible mark, shaping the souls of those who simply wish to be held and understood.

It is vital to understand that this parenting approach may be an unconscious pattern passed down from generation to generation, where adults who were raised in a similar manner unknowingly perpetuate the cycle. Those caregivers whose children develop an ambivalent attachment style are often prone to possess an anxious attachment style themselves. This is not a matter of genetics but rather the continuous transmission of behavioral patterns through the generations. But dear reader, cycles are broken, and that is the magic in being mindful. We'll learn about ways to do this as we continue on.

ANXIOUS LOVE

In the realm of attachment, one finds the anxious soul navigating a terrain shaped by an overwhelming desire to please others, perpetually haunted by the fear of rejection and the terror of being left behind. This attachment style emerges from the ashes of an unpredictable childhood, where caregivers were often absent, rather than abusive.

Such inconsistency compels individuals to remain perpetually vigilant and apprehensive of abandonment. As the subconscious mind absorbs the patterns it's consistently exposed to, it gradually constructs a framework centered around the fear of being forsaken. Given that fear of abandonment is among the few intrinsic fears, inconsistent parenting relentlessly fuels anxiety in the child, fostering a deep-rooted sense of desertion.

People often react to challenging circumstances by putting their own adult needs aside, subconsciously trying to maintain relationships. They might start giving too much of themselves in friendships and romantic partnerships to avoid potential rejection, which inevitably leads to a simmering resentment. Often, the cause of this struggle is the blurred line between making reasonable compromises and making sacrifices that ignore their own needs completely. They find it difficult to distinguish between temporary adjustments and complete neglect of their needs, setting the stage for long-term disappointment and unhappiness. This inner conflict keeps building until it becomes overwhelming, leading to a point of emotional collapse.

In the progression of time, those burdened with anxious attachment may find themselves entangled in unwholesome patterns, confronting a diminished sense of self-worth, and bearing the ruins of collapsed relationships. They dwell on their missteps for years, weeks, days, but seldom do they address the crux of the matter, the very miscommunications that lie at the heart of it all. Yet, these emotions, born from the primal wounds of anxious attachment, are far from irreparable. Embraced by relationships steeped in validation, presence, and a gentle warmth, these individuals have the potential to flourish as extraordinary partners and fully come into their own.[41]

WHAT DOES ANXIOUS ATTACHMENT LOOK LIKE?

We've all seen what anxious attachment looks like. Maybe without knowing what it is!

Think about Bella Swan from the movie "Twilight": Bella's anxious attachment reveals itself in her hunger for reassurance and the gnawing fear of being abandoned by Edward. She even ventures into perilous situations just to feel closer to him. Bella's journey to resolution involves embracing her newfound life as a vampire and cultivating self-assurance, which paves the way for a healthier relationship with Edward, one founded on mutual trust and understanding.

These types of individuals possess an acute awareness of everything their significant other is doing, thinking, and they want to be one step ahead to accommodate. Though they often wrestle with feelings of insecurity and doubt about their own importance in the relationship. Should their loved one dismiss or overlook their needs, they may internalize blame or consider themselves unworthy of love. For the most part people with anxious attachment crave ongoing validation of their worth, loveability, and competence. To the point, sometimes, that it obviously pushes people away. It may even present as though the anxious individual is self-obsessed, when really, they just want to be understood and loved.

The strong fear of being left behind often causes deep jealousy or doubt towards their partners in anxious adults. Think of Clara and her need for attention from her peers. These feelings lead to unpredictable actions that might seem strange to someone with a more stable way of connecting with others; like Clara's lashing out at her party. This worry may also show itself as a sense of urgency, clinginess, and focus on their relationships. This can result in doing things for the wrong reasons which have dire consequences. Anxiously attached people are often scared of, or even unable to handle, being alone. They look for closeness and rightfully so, showing strong emotions and depending on others. For them, having a loved one nearby seems to be the answer to their big emotional needs.[42]

NAVIGATION TECHNIQUES

Navigating a relationship with someone who has an anxious attachment style is a complex dance of intimacy and vulnerability. To cultivate a healthy and satisfying partnership, one must be aware of the potential challenges and benefits, and learn to gracefully manage the intricacies of anxious attachment.

Challenges

Longing for reassurance: Individuals with anxious attachment often hunger for continuous affirmation and reassurance of their partner's love and commitment. This can be emotionally taxing for their partners.

Mistrust and jealousy: Anxious attachment can breed heightened jealousy and suspicion, which may lead to conflicts and misunderstandings.

Emotional dependency: Anxiously attached partners may become excessively reliant on their significant others, creating an imbalance in the relationship and stifling personal growth for both individuals.

Abandonment fears: The potent fear of being abandoned can prompt controlling or manipulative behaviors in an effort to preserve the relationship, potentially fostering tension and resentment.

Benefits

Emotional resonance: Anxiously attached individuals are often attuned to their partners' needs and emotions, fostering a deep emotional connection.

Nurturing and support: People with anxious attachment can be very caring and supportive, as they are heavily invested in their relationships.

Steadfast commitment: Anxiously attached partners are typically devoted to making their relationships work and are often very loyal.

STRATEGIES FOR COMMUNICATION AND MANAGING ANXIOUS ATTACHMENT

Therapy: Encourage your partner to seek professional help, such as individual or couples therapy, to address attachment issues and develop healthier coping strategies.

Self-reflection: Both partners should engage in self-reflection to understand their own attachment patterns and how they may contribute to relationship dynamics.

Honest communication: Maintain open and candid communication about feelings, needs, and expectations. This can help build trust and alleviate anxiety for the anxiously attached partner.

Reliability: Provide consistent and predictable support to help assuage your partner's fears of abandonment and enhance their sense of security in the relationship.

Active listening: Demonstrate empathy and understanding by actively listening to your partner's concerns and validating their emotions.

Boundaries: Establish and maintain healthy boundaries to ensure both partners' needs are met and the relationship remains balanced.

Conflict resolution: Tackle conflicts constructively, concentrating on finding solutions and understanding each other's perspectives rather than assigning blame.

By recognizing the challenges and benefits of being in a relationship with an anxiously attached partner and employing effective communication and management strategies, it's possible to build a robust, supportive, and fulfilling partnership.

HEALING TECHNIQUES

There are many techniques that can help an anxious person become more secure. Combined with the skills we've talked about in the last chapter, distress tolerance and emotional regulation (see healing techniques in next chapter, too!) are especially important for those with an anxious attachment style. Remember, all of the healing techniques are useful for every insecure attachment type, be it avoidant, disorganized, and of course, anxious.

Acceptance and Commitment Therapy (ACT) is a form of psychotherapy that combines mindfulness and acceptance strategies with commitment and behavior change techniques. The primary goal of ACT is to increase psychological flexibility, enabling individuals to respond more effectively to life's challenges.

Below are examples of ACT activities that can deliver some of the benefits of this form of psychotherapy. In your Workbook you'll see these activities listed with guidance on how to conduct them yourself. So, read below and then, if you feel these may be relevant to you or your partner, turn to your Workbook and perform the activities.

Imagine you're an intrepid explorer on a quest to conquer the anxiously attached dragon. Your first stop? The land of Values. This is where you'll jot down your personal values like a treasure map. Think about what really rocks your boat in different areas of your life - relationships, work, personal growth - the works!

Next, you'll journey into the labyrinth of Avoidance Patterns. Be like an archaeologist, dig up those behaviors you've been using to dodge anxiety and fear of rejection. Remember how you always 'forget' to reply to a text when you sense conflict brewing? Bingo! That's an avoidance pattern.

Now, it's time to tune into Mindfulness FM. This is your go-to station for staying present and keeping track of your thoughts, emotions, and body sensations without getting judgy. Deep breathing, body scanning, meditation - these are all your mindfulness mixtapes. And hey, don't sweat it! We'll dive deeper into this in the following chapters.

Next up, we've got Cognitive Defusion. This isn't a fancy physics term, but it's just as cool. It's about learning to see your thoughts as chatty neighbors rather than unshakeable truths. Just observe them gossiping away without getting sucked into the drama. Remember, thoughts are just thoughts, not stone-cold facts.

Ah, Acceptance! This one's a biggie. It's about embracing your feelings, thoughts, and experiences like they're all invited to your party, even the not-so-pleasant ones. Give yourself a pat on the back, and remember that having all kinds of emotions is just being human.

Now, Commitment. This is where you pledge to act according to your values, even when it feels as tough as chewing on a rubber boot. Set specific goals and baby-step your way towards them, like deciding to express your needs more assertively in your relationships.

Lastly, we're at Behavior Change. This is where you start flexing your newfound skills. Improving your communication, setting boundaries, or creating new coping strategies for dealing with anxiety and fear of rejection - these are your power moves. Practice them, and you'll be well on your way to building healthier relationships and slaying that anxiously attached beast!

The following text is repeated and expanded in your Workbook with space for your own written reflections and recorded actions.

Using ACT for an anxiously attached person involves the following steps:

1. **Identify values**: Clarify your personal values and what matters most to them in various areas of your life, such as relationships, work, and personal growth.

2. **Recognize anxious patterns**: Identify anxious behaviors and understand how these patterns have developed as a coping mechanism for dealing with emotional triggers and fear of rejection.

3. **Mindfulness**: Master mindfulness techniques to help you become more aware of your thoughts, emotions,

and physical sensations in the present moment without judgment. This can include practices such as deep breathing, body scanning, and meditation. We will delve further into mindfulness techniques in the following chapters.

4. **Cognitive defusion**: Learn to distance yourself from your thoughts and not treat them as absolute truths. Techniques for cognitive defusion may include observing thoughts without engaging with them or labeling thoughts as just thoughts rather than facts.

5. **Acceptance:** Accept your feelings, thoughts, and experiences without trying to change or avoid them. This involves practicing self-compassion and recognizing that emotions, even difficult ones, are a natural part of life.

6. **Commitment**: Make a commitment to act in accordance with their values, even if it means facing anxiety or discomfort. This can include setting specific goals and taking small, manageable steps towards achieving them.

7. **Behavior change**: Implement new behaviors that align with your values and help to build healthier relationships. This may involve improving communication skills, setting boundaries, or developing new coping strategies for dealing with anxiety and fear of rejection.

By incorporating these steps, ACT can help anxiously attached individuals become more flexible in their thinking, accept their emotions, and ultimately, take actions that align with their values and lead to more fulfilling relationships.[43]

CONCLUSION

To sum up, the root of anxious attachment lies in the erratic nature of parental care, leaving individuals a profound, lingering dread of abandonment and spurning. This sense of uncertainty infiltrates various aspects of adult life, shaping romantic entanglements, friendships, and one's overall self-esteem. Comprehending one's attachment style and pondering its repercussions on their existence is pivotal to individual evolution and the formation of healthier connections.

In this chapter, we have delved into the anxious attachment style, scrutinized its influence on relationships, and examined its bearing on communication and emotional management. It is of utmost importance to acknowledge that the path to healing is attainable, and by nurturing relationships filled with validation, presence, and warmth, individuals can cultivate a more secure attachment style.

I ask you, dear reader, to contemplate your own attachment style and assess its sway over your relationships. Through fostering self-awareness, you can embark on the journey to develop a more secure attachment style, ultimately participating in more wholesome, gratifying relationships. Bear in mind that insight and growth are the essentials to shattering the cycle and forging a future that embraces profound bonds and meaningful memories.

In our next chapter, we'll see how disorganized attachment can be a push an pull between all of the aforementioned styles. We'll learn how to cope with this and perhaps understand loved ones with this attachment style.

7

HOW TRAUMA RAVAGES RELATIONSHIPS IN DISORGANIZED ATTACHMENT

We've covered a lot. The final attachment style may be the most difficult to wrap one's mind around; disorganized attachment. Disorganized attachment, a form of insecure attachment, takes root in childhood and echoes through the relationships one encounters throughout life. It is marked by a fragmented pattern of attachment, where people exhibit contradictory or confused responses to stress. Disorganized attachment has been connected to numerous mental health concerns, and has even emerged as a crucial element in the therapeutic treatment of patients grappling with borderline personality disorder.[44] While various tools exist to evaluate attachment styles, such as Adult Attachment Styles, none of them seem to accurately capture the essence of disorganization.[45] Research has also delved into the interplay between genetic and environmental factors in shaping the development of disorganized attachment.

Navigating through life with a disorganized attachment style is an intricate dance of inconsistency and emotional turbulence. Rooted in childhood, this form of insecure attachment often emerges from experiences steeped in adversity, such as abuse or social exclusion. While uncommon in the wider population, it is a pattern more prevalent among children under state care.

Individuals with disorganized attachment struggle with complex emotions, entwining conflicting dependence and hostility or fear towards others. Disorganized people often navigate relationships with a peculiar ambivalence, oscillating between vulnerability and distance. This attachment style is closely tied to various mental health challenges and holds significant importance in addressing borderline personality disorder in therapy. Though these attachment patterns may linger, the potential for change remains, provided the right intervention and support are in place. Such behavior pervades all types of relationships. They tend to be over analytical focusing on the negative in relationships and conflicts that arise. As we've talked about earlier in the book, this is rooted in an untrusting childhood relationship with their parents—perhaps due to many factors like addiction or emotional instability—these individuals scrutinize, replay conversations, look for cues that someone may or may not like them, silently judging expressions and words through social interactions.[46]

RELATIONSHIPS WITH THE DISORGANIZED INDIVIDUAL

Disorganized attachment style can greatly affect relationships. People with this attachment style may have difficulty forming and keeping healthy relationships because of inconsistent behavior and mixed responses to stress. They might also experience complex emotional issues, like conflicting dependency patterns and feelings of anger or fear towards others. With trust not coming naturally, they remain ever vigilant against the possibility of being deceived. The central wounds of this attachment style encompass feelings of unworthiness, exploitation, and a lack of safety. This unpredictability often stems from a childhood marked by moments of abuse and emotional support, breeding an inherent sense of confusion and distrust. Consequently, they yearn for love while anticipating betrayal, causing immense internal conflict. Studies show that disorganized attachment can lead to anxiety disorders later in life. [47]

Those with a disorganized attachment style want what everyone else wants; to be loved, and understood. But often, it's possible that the negative experiences of those with this attachment style hinder the acceptance of love. They can often project deceit, frustration, and ambivalence onto relationships. Dating someone with a disorganized attachment style can be stressful, due to their own stressful responses to situations. They often have trouble regulating their emotions and suffer from profound anxiety attacks.[48,49]

DYNAMICS OF A RELATIONSHIP WITH A DISORGANIZED INDIVIDUAL

In the quaint coastal town where Elise and Ben lived, love seemed to be a delicate and unpredictable thing. They met during their first year of university and quickly became inseparable. Ben was drawn to Elise's intelligence and wit, while she found comfort in his warmth and understanding. Their connection was undeniable, yet it was also marred by the complexities of Elise's disorganized attachment style.

As their relationship progressed, Elise found it increasingly difficult to open up emotionally to Ben. She longed for the deep connection they shared in the beginning, but the fear of vulnerability held her back. Ben would try to engage her in meaningful conversations, only to be met with her sudden withdrawal, leaving him feeling helpless and disconnected from the woman he loved.

Elise's fears of abandonment haunted her every day. Even though Ben had never given her a reason to doubt his commitment, her insecurities gnawed at her incessantly. She would text and call him obsessively, seeking constant reassurance of his love for her. Ben did his best to assuage her fears, but the weight of her clinginess soon began to wear on him, making him crave space from the very person he wanted to be close to.

Their love was a paradox, a map of affection and conflict held together by the threads of Elise's disorganized attachment. One moment, she would be loving and tender, and the next, a storm of anger and fear would erupt, leaving Ben bewildered and disheartened. Simple conversations would often escalate into heated arguments as Elise accused him of not caring about her or wanting to leave the relationship.

The push-pull dynamic between them was a constant source of confusion and frustration. Elise would initiate intimate moments, only to retreat as soon as Ben responded with the same affection. He never knew how to navigate her conflicting signals, and it left them both feeling emotionally exhausted.

Trust was another casualty of Elise's past experiences. She struggled to believe in Ben's intentions, creating a cycle of suspicion and insecurity that made it difficult for them to build a solid foundation. Misunderstandings and disagreements became commonplace, and the once blissful couple found themselves at a crossroads.

Recognizing the need for change, Elise and Ben decided to seek therapy, where they learned about disorganized attachment and its effects on their relationship. Through open communication and the guidance of a skilled therapist, they began to address the underlying issues that fueled their struggles.

As they embarked on their journey of healing, Elise and Ben learned that love, though fragile and unpredictable, could be resilient and enduring. With patience, understanding, and a commitment to growth, they worked together to develop healthier patterns of attachment, slowly unraveling the tangled web of emotions that had once held them captive. In the end, their love emerged stronger and more secure, a testament to the power of understanding and the indestructable human spirit.

HEALING TECHNIQUES

Mindfulness techniques can help everyone, and I will have an entire chapter dedicated to those useful tools later in the book. But, for those with disorganized attachment styles, let's focus on **emotional regulation** tools.

Part of the struggle in regulating our emotions is checking in on our subconscious beliefs. These are the ideas programmed within our deep beings, ideas we don't even know exist. Thais Gibson notes in their book about attachment styles that 90% of our thoughts are subconscious. Gibson labels these "automatic thoughts". To deal with these let's move on to checking the facts.[49b]

CHECK THE FACTS

The "Check the Facts" tool, developed by Dr. Marsha M. Linehan, is a skill used to help individuals evaluate their thoughts and emotions in relation to a specific situation. By examining the facts of the situation and assessing whether their thoughts and feelings are justified, individuals can gain a clearer perspective and make more informed decisions. This process involves identifying emotions, considering possible interpretations of events, and then determining if there is evidence to support these interpretations.

By checking the facts, individuals can better regulate their emotions and respond more effectively to situations.

How do you do this? You ask? Well, turn to your Workbook where the text below is repeated with space to complete each exercise.

1. Identify the target emotion: Ask yourself, "What is the emotion I want to change?" This helps you focus on the specific emotion you're experiencing and wish to address.

2. Pinpoint the triggering event: Ask, "What is the event prompting my emotion?" By identifying the event or situation that triggered the emotion, you can start examining its context and your reaction to it.

3. Analyze interpretations and thoughts: Ask, "What are my interpretations, thoughts, and assumptions about the event?" This step encourages you to explore the thoughts and beliefs that contribute to your emotional reaction.

4. Assess potential threats: Ask, "Am I assuming a threat?" Evaluate whether you perceive a real, immediate, or significant threat to your well-being, values, or self-image in the situation.

5. Identify the catastrophe: Ask, "What's the catastrophe?" Determine the worst-case scenario that may be fueling your emotional reaction, and assess whether it's a realistic possibility.

6. Evaluate the fit between emotion and facts: Ask, "Does my emotion and/or its intensity fit the actual facts?" Assess if your emotional reaction is appropriate and proportional to

the situation, based on the information available and the context in which it occurred.

CONCLUSION

In this chapter, we delved into disorganized attachment, a complex style influenced by childhood adversity such as abuse or social exclusion. This attachment style manifests itself in relationships through contradictory behaviors, as individuals grapple with a desire for closeness and simultaneous fear of vulnerability. Disorganized attachment is linked to mental health challenges, including anxiety disorders and borderline personality disorder. With understanding, patience, and therapeutic interventions like mindfulness and emotional regulation tools, individuals can work towards healthier connections, addressing their internal conflicts and developing secure attachments. Love, though vulnerable to life's uncertainties, can grow stronger through this process, showcasing the resilience of the human spirit. We'll now learn how to transfer understanding oneself to creating a world of love in chapter 8.

HOW UNDERSTANDING YOURSELF CAN REVOLUTIONIZE YOUR RELATIONSHIPS

Everything That Matters Is Within

People have (with the help of conventions) oriented all their solutions toward the easy and toward the easiest side of the easy; but it is clear that we must hold to what is difficult; everything alive holds to it."

– Raianer Maria Rilke

One morning in Seattle, under the cover of rain, Marianne woke up to the echo of emptiness. She felt an ennui so profound it seemed to seep from her bones. The city outside her window was shrouded in grey, matching the color of her mood. It was as though she was living in a perpetual state of dusk. The departure of her girlfriend had left her fragmented, and the death of her father seemed to further the fractures.

Marianne had always had a disorganized attachment style; her relationships were a patchwork of longing and emotional aloofness. She yearned for closeness, but it also terrified her. This cycle of craving and fear was exhausting, and she was too tired to keep fighting it.

Her job at the library archives was her refuge. Surrounded by the quiet rustling of papers and the scent of old books, she sought solace in the organization of history, a stark contrast to her inner turmoil. With each document she archived, she found a sense of order, a fleeting moment of control, and a tangible accomplishment.

On days she felt especially unmoored, she asked a friend what her options were. It was hard to ask for help. Together they determined she could: a.) roll over and die b.) seek further help beyond her therapist c.) Let her emptiness find a permanent home in her life. She asked her therapist about group therapy and other options. Her therapist directed her to DBT and mindfulness practices. She met the group twice a week. It was hard work, and it demanded consistent thoughtfulness and daily practice. But., they were the tools she used to dismantle her grief, breaking it into smaller pieces she could manage. She learned to observe her feelings without judgment, noting their presence like clouds passing in the sky. Mindfulness was a gentle reminder that she was more than her pain.

She was recently sober. Most days she woke up and still felt like garbage. A friend reminded her that, even though she felt hollow, it could be far worse if she were still drinking. This decision alienated her from her peer group. But she had realized upon the loss of her dad that if she wanted to retain a semblance of control, drinking was not an option. All of this, the loss of her dad, girlfriend, and dealing with an addiction, compounded, felt overwhelming. All she could do was take every day as it came. One day at a time.

Her other source of comfort was her dog, Bailey. Their hikes in the Cascades were cathartic, a testament to the healing power of nature. The rhythm of their footsteps on the trail, the breath of the forest, the whispers of the wind - all helped her find a sense of calm amidst the chaos of her emotions.

One day, as Marianne and Bailey reached a peak overlooking the city, she took a deep breath, tasting the crisp air. She realized she was beginning to feel lighter, as if she were gradually shedding a heavy coat she'd been wearing for too long. Her heart still ached, but it was no longer a gaping wound.

Marianne understood that she was on a journey of convalescence into wholeness. It was a solitary journey, filled with moments of despair and flickers of hope. But she was beginning to accept that she could be alone without being lonely, that she could be whole without being untouched by sorrow.

Sorrow was something she could work with. Like clay, she could mold it into something useful. Wield her depths of despair and sensitivity into a beautiful understanding. She began to realize that somehow, this was all a gift.

As she stood there, looking at the city below, she realized that she was like Seattle itself. She was capable of weathering storms, of existing under clouds, of living in the shadow of mountains. And like Seattle, she too had the promise of beautiful days ahead, of vibrant blooms after the rain, of light breaking through the gray.

The path to healing wasn't linear. There were days when she woke up and didn't feel like going on. But on those days, she reminded herself that she had survived 100% of her worst days, and this was just another day she would survive.

Her father was gone. Her girlfriend was gone. But Marianne was still here - breathing, living, healing. She had her job, her dog, her hikes, her mindfulness practices. She had herself. And that was something. That was everything.

THE IMPORTANCE OF RECOGNIZING ONE'S OWN ATTACHMENT STYLE

Recognizing one's own attachment style is a journey of self-understanding. It's about peering into our emotional blueprints, seeing how we connect, how we love, and how we react to intimacy and its loss. It's an exploration that, often, is as illuminating as it is uncomfortable.

An anxious attachment style manifests as a deep-seated fear of abandonment. This fear can turn love into a battlefield, marked by constant vigilance for signs of rejection. Healing here is not about suppressing this anxiety but rather about learning to hold it lightly. It's about understanding that love is not a scarce resource that will vanish at the slightest mistake. Healing is the journey from a world of scarcity to a world of abundance.

Then there's the avoidant attachment style, characterized by a strong desire for independence, often at the expense of intimacy. It's a defensive stance, a fortress built around the heart. Yet, behind this fortress lies a fear of engulfment, a fear of losing oneself in another. Healing here is about realizing that connection doesn't mean dissolution. It's about learning that one can be a part of a whole without losing their individuality.

A disorganized attachment style is perhaps the most painful. It's a tangle of contradictions - a longing for closeness paired with a terror of it. The core wound here is often rooted in early experiences of chaos and unpredictability. Healing is a process of learning to find stability within oneself, of transforming inner chaos into inner calm. It's about understanding that the past doesn't have to dictate the future.

And finally, secure attachment, the holy grail of attachment styles. It's a state of comfort with both intimacy and independence. But it's not about perfection. It's about resilience. It's about being able to navigate the ebb and flow of closeness and distance, to soothe oneself and to seek comfort from others. The beauty of secure attachment is that it's not a birthright, but a possibility, a destination that can be reached with understanding, patience, and kindness towards oneself.

Recognizing one's attachment style is not about assigning blame, but about gaining awareness. It's not about fixing oneself, but about nurturing oneself. Because healing is not a destination, it's a journey. It's a journey of understanding our patterns, of untangling our fears, of learning to love in a way that feels safe, secure, and fulfilling. And it's a journey that is entirely, beautifully, achingly human.

SELF ASSESSMENT

Below you'll find a self-assessment to find your attachment style. For every question, mark the amount of points and add them together at the end. These questions are repeated in the Workbook with space to record your answers and tally your score. You'll also see the 'Attachment Style' that corresponds to your final tally shown in the Workbook.

Question 1: Are you in a relationship?

>   a. Yes (+1 point)

>   b. No (0 points)

Question 2: What is your relationship status?

>   a. Short-term relationship (less than one year) (0 points)

>   b. Long-term relationship (more than one year) (+1 point)

>   c. Married (+2 points)

Question 3: How would you rate your current satisfaction in your relationship?

a. We're very happy (+2 points)

b. Things are not how I would like them to be (+1 point)

Question 4: When it comes to emotional presence with others (friends, family, partners), it takes me some time to build trust and feel comfortable sharing vulnerable aspects of myself.

a. True (+1 point)

b. False (0 points)

Question 5: I often place significant importance on the people in my life (partners, friends, family), viewing them in an idealized way or putting them on a pedestal.

a. True (+1 point)

b. False (0 points)

Question 6: I feel at ease expressing my feelings and needs to loved ones, finding it natural and comfortable to do so.

a. True (+1 point)

b. False (0 points)

Question 7: I experience a strong sense of distress when others encroach upon my need for personal space or time alone.

a. True (+1 point)

b. False (0 points)

Question 8: I am inclined to work through challenges in a relationship rather than abruptly ending it, displaying a commitment to resolving conflicts. (If you're not in a relationship, consider how you handle conflicts in partnerships.)

    a. True (+1 point)

    b. False (0 points)

Question 9: I often feel disconnected from my emotions, finding it challenging to stay in touch with them frequently.

    a. True (0 points)

    b. False (+1 point)

Question 10: I tend to be highly attuned to the needs of others, often prioritizing them over my own and later experiencing resentment.

    a. True (0 points)

    b. False (+1 point)

Question 11: I consistently desire greater emotional closeness with my partner, as well as in my close friendships or romantic interests.

    a. True (+1 point)

    b. False (0 points)

Question 12: I am effective at compromising and communicating within relationships, demonstrating skill and effectiveness in these areas.

    a. True (+1 point)

    b. False (0 points)

Question 13: Setting boundaries can be quite challenging for me unless I am angry. At times, I may establish excessive boundaries and push people away dramatically when angry.

> a. True (0 points)

> b. False (+1 point)

Question 14: If I observe signs of coldness from my partner, I tend to experience panic and an immediate urge to get closer as quickly as possible. This pattern is also evident in my friendships.

> a. True (+1 point)

> b. False (0 points)

Question 15: Experiencing inward emotional turbulence throughout the course of my romantic relationship, as well as with close family members, is not uncommon for me.

> a. True (+1 point)

> b. False (0 points)

Question 16: I frequently oscillate between intense warmth and coldness towards my partner or family members, often operating in extremes when relating to others.

> a. True (0 points)

> b. False (+1 point)

Question 17: I have a strong belief in my own worthiness of a healthy and happy relationship.

> a. True (+1 point)

> b. False (0 points)

Question 18: What is your primary motivation for learning about attachment theory?

    a. To gain a better understanding of myself (+1 point)

    b. To gain a better understanding of my partner (+1 point)

Question 19: When I feel hurt by a loved one, I often experience a strong fight or flight response, wanting to push them away as far as possible (friends, family, romantic relationships).

    a. True (+1 point)

    b. False (0 points)

Question 20: I do not feel as though I need anything from my romantic partner or loved ones. It can be difficult to conceptualize how others would meet a lot of my needs.

    a. True (0 points)

    b. False (+1 point)

Question 21: I do not enjoy being without romantic relationships. I often fear being alone.

    a. True (+1 point)

    b. False (0 points)

Question 22: When a loved one's behavior hurts me, I make an effort to express my feelings and try to understand what caused them to act that way.

    a. True (+1 point)

    b. False (0 points)

Question 23: I long for emotional closeness, but I also fear the emotional difficulty that comes with it in relationships with friends, family, and romantic partners.

    a. True (+1 point)

    b. False (0 points)

Question 24: I do not prefer making social plans with others in advance as I often fear being trapped by commitments with other people.

    a. True (0 points)

    b. False (+1 point)

Question 25: Setting boundaries comes naturally to me.

    a. True (+1 point)

    b. False (0 points)

Question 26: I tend to focus more on the relationships in my life than on myself.

    a. True (0 points)

    b. False (+1 point)

Question 27: I often feel protective over my space, privacy, and belongings.

    a. True (+1 point)

    b. False (0 points)

Question 28: Generally, I feel invaded when my partner or loved ones demand too much physical affection.

    a. True (+1 point)

    b. False (0 points)

Question 29: If I were to be in a romantic relationship, I would prefer to spend most of my free time with my partner. It would be hard for me to want to do things separately.

    a. True (+1 point)

    b. False (0 points)

Question 30: I find it easy to be vulnerable with my romantic partner or loved ones.

    a. True (+1 point)

    b. False (0 points)

Question 31: I often find that my partner or loved ones emotionally recover from conflicts before I do.

    a. True (0 points)

    b. False (+1 point)

Question 32: I experience a deep fear of being abandoned by my partner or love interests.

    a. True (+1 point)

    b. False (0 points)

Question 33: How familiar are you with attachment theory?

>   a. This is my first time hearing about it (0 points)

>   b. I know a little bit (+1 point)

>   c. I feel well versed in it (+2 points)

>   d. I consider myself an expert on it (+3 points)

Armed with knowing your attachment style, we continue on in chapter 9 to map out how to work this knowledge into a better love life.

THE BLUEPRINT FOR YOUR LOVE LIFE

The Attachment You're Asking For And How To Get It

Love doesn't cling; it frees. Healthy attachment in love is knowing that you are distinct, that the one you love can leave, but you are content knowing they choose to stay.

A great tumult echoes within us, a testament to our first guardians, the patterns of feelings and expectations drawn from our opening chapters with those we first called caregivers. A dance of need and care, a mirror for our deepest self, it is here that our attachment styles take root.

In the terrain of the Securely Attached, the caregiver is the dependable sun, a constant presence that offers warmth and nurturing. This child, cradled in the reliability of their caregiver's attention, learns to navigate their world confidently, seeking out new frontiers while anchored in the knowledge of their caregiver's steadfast presence. As they weave themselves into the tapestry of adulthood, this early molding transforms into relationships that echo those first feelings of safety and interdependence, a dance of reliance and self-sufficiency. In the realm of love, they may sail with confidence, offering their partners an unflinching loyalty and a stable, nourishing presence.

Yet not all caretakers are suns. In the anxious child's world, the caregiver is the mercurial moon, their illumination inconsistent and changing. This child can never predict when the light of care will shine or fade, and so they cling. As adults, these children-turned-men-and-women often find themselves in a constant dance of anxiety and desire in their romantic engagements, longing for their lovers with an intensity that seeks to ensure constant proximity and the elusive reassurance that the moon won't fade again.

Then there are the children of the Avoidant Attachment, whose caregiver was more like the distant stars - observable, but largely unresponsive. These children learn to turn inwards, cultivating a rugged self-reliance. As adults, they bring this self-contained universe into their romantic relationships, creating a constellation of emotional distance and autonomy. For their lovers, the challenge is in crossing these vast expanses, in persuading the star to drop its solitary act and share its sky.

The world of the Disorganized Attachment child is a paradox, their caregiver both a source of terror and comfort - a frightening comet that leaves a trail of fear. As these children evolve into adults, they often move unpredictably in relationships, alternating between the anxious need for closeness and the avoidant impulse to self-protect. Their romantic relationships may become a battlefield of unresolved conflicts, an echo of their early chaos.

But these constellations of our early attachments are not our destiny. They can be observed, understood, and transformed over time, with new experiences, relationships, and therapy. Like celestial bodies in motion, we too can change our course, realign our orbits. The key is recognizing the patterns and understanding their gravitational pull on our relationships. Therapy, in this cosmic dance, can serve as a guide, illuminating our path and helping us navigate towards healthier ways of relating to others.

YOUR LOVE LIFE AND YOUR PAST LIFE

There is a case study conducted by theorists Dorota Iwaniec and Helga Sneddon that involved following the lives of children with FTT (failure to thrive disorder). Failure to Thrive (FTT) is a term used in pediatric medicine to refer to children who are significantly below the normal weight or rate of weight gain for their age. While it's most often applied to infants and toddlers, older children can also experience FTT.[50]

FTT is not a specific disease or disorder itself, but rather a sign that a child is undernourished or not gaining enough weight for a variety of possible reasons. These can include medical conditions, psychosocial factors like neglect or abuse, or a combination of both. It's important to identify and address the underlying cause, as chronic malnutrition can have lasting effects on a child's growth and cognitive development.

Over a span of twenty years, researchers spent time examining their childhood environments, attachment styles, and the transformations that ensued over time. This study compared their adult attachment styles with the ones they had established with their mothers during their childhood. It concluded that "internal working models" (refer to chapter 2) can undergo changes when provided with appropriate support, intervention, or when different relationships or circumstances are encountered.

It is commonly understood that one's attachment style with their primary caregiver plays a significant role in shaping their future attachments, particularly in romantic relationships. Iwaniec and Sneddon concur that these "internal working models" can be self-perpetuating as individuals tend to gravitate towards environments that align with their self-perception and worldview.

However, they emphasize that these models are not set in stone. In the context of love and romantic relationships, their research suggests that exposure to a positive and healthy intimate relationship can foster a sense of security in individuals previously categorized as insecure (anxious, disorganized, avoidant). Conversely, a secure person could become insecure following a negative intimate experience. Furthermore, the study posits that a person's internal working models can be adjusted when they reflect upon and understand their past attachment patterns.

Initially, among the 31 children in the study, 14 were identified as having a secure attachment style, nine showed signs of anxious attachment, and eight exhibited avoidant behavior. However, as these children matured into adults, their attachment classifications notably evolved.

In adulthood, the number of individuals with secure attachment significantly rose from 14 to 22.

The anxious category shrank dramatically from nine children to just a single adult. Interestingly, while the count of those with avoidant attachment remained at eight, the actual individuals in this category had changed from childhood.

The majority of participants who were categorized as securely attached during their childhood maintained this attachment style into adulthood, with a total of 13 individuals. All of these participants were the result of planned pregnancies, a detail we'll delve into later as it may contribute to these transitions from childhood to adulthood.

One participant who was categorized as secure during childhood exhibited an avoidant attachment style in adulthood. This individual's life was marked by several traumatic events, including enduring mental illness and the suicide of her father.

Most of the people who were avoidant as children were also avoidant as adults (5 out of 8).

Three children who initially exhibited avoidant attachment styles transitioned to secure attachment styles in adulthood. Two of these individuals were relocated from their emotionally distressing home environments and placed into stable, long-term foster care. The third child experienced improved conditions when their mother left an unhealthy relationship with the child's father and embarked on a positive relationship with a new partner. These transformations underscore how changes in caregivers or home situations can foster emotionally secure and stable environments for children, thereby influencing their attachment styles.

One individual who displayed anxious attachment as a child maintained this pattern into adulthood. Two previously anxious children developed avoidant attachment styles when they became adults. However, the majority of the once anxious children, six in total, transitioned into secure attachment in their adult lives.

"One of these children was adopted at a very early age and three children were fostered out long term. One child remained in the home environment and showed improvement when her mother's new partner moved in (as above). The other two children remained in the home environment throughout intervention.

The researchers attribute the long-term changes to the following:

1.   Natural changes in attachment patterns

2.   The interventions (See below)

3.   Change in quality of parenting

4.   Temperamental factors and cognitive abilities

5.   Other undecided factors.

The intervention included help with economic matters, allowances, counseling for parents (which was required) and this involved cognitive restructuring and marital therapy.

"The therapeutic elements of the intervention usually involved a few stages:

1. Modifying maternal behavior and responses during breastfeeding.

2. Attachment work: increasing positive interactions between members of the family which could include, play sessions, improved communication, exposure to physical togetherness, story reading, touching, kissing, speaking softly and encouragingly.

3. Intensifying of mother–child interactions;

4. Some older children with a long history of FTT present behavioral problems: these were dealt with once the 'emotional arousal' in the family (especially between mother and child) improved;

5. Group work for mothers of FTT children."[51]

Several developmental theorists propose that adults naturally reassess their relationships in response to significant life events or changing conditions. Take, for instance, someone becoming a parent for the first time. This transformation could lead to a renewed or more profound comprehension of their bond with their own parents. As a result, they might attain a more cohesive understanding of themselves and others. This process could alter their perspective on their attachment relationships, their assessment of their original family, or even both.

In conclusion, the study conducted by Dorota Iwaniec and Helga Sneddon substantiates the notion that change in attachment style throughout adulthood is not only possible but also somewhat expected, given the shifts in life circumstances and personal growth. While the impact of early childhood attachment is undeniably significant in shaping one's relationships and worldview, the inherent fluidity of these attachment styles is evident.

The observations drawn from the life trajectories of children with FTT underscore the resilience and adaptability of human behavior in response to shifts in environmental and interpersonal dynamics. Changes in the quality of care, the stability of the home environment, and substantial therapeutic interventions can significantly contribute to altering an individual's attachment patterns. Furthermore, personal introspection and understanding of past attachment styles can enable self-guided evolution of these patterns.

The transition of anxious children into secure adults, in particular, serves as a compelling testament to the fact that attachment styles are not a life sentence. Similarly, the changes observed in secure and avoidant children/adults highlight that attachment patterns are not immutable and can be reshaped by experiences, relationships, and personal growth.

Therefore, this research strongly supports the view that individuals are not destined to remain within the bounds of their early attachment styles. Given appropriate support, intervention, or changing life circumstances, individuals can navigate their way towards healthier and more secure attachment styles. This dynamism of attachment styles offers a promising perspective for those seeking to improve their relationships and personal development. This revelation certainly brings a ray of hope for everyone![52]

HOW DIFFERENT ATTACHMENT STYLES WORK TOGETHER IN ROMANCE

In the realm of the secure attached, two people find each other, their hearts open and responsive. They hold up mirrors to each other, reflecting positivity. Their words intertwine in effective communication, their emotions play out in the open, and their conflicts find a balanced resolution. They dance a dance of respect for independence, while also holding hands in moments of need. They form a symphony of intimacy and autonomy.

When secure meets anxious, stability enters the scene through the secure's adeptness at handling conflicts and communication. This steady hand can soothe the anxious heart, calming its fear of rejection or abandonment. Yet, the constant pulse of reassurance that the anxious requires may sometimes overwhelm the rhythm of the secure. Here, understanding becomes a bridge, and effective communication, the path across it.

Secure and avoidant? That's another story. The secure, a constant presence, a beacon of understanding, can coax the avoidant into the warmth of intimacy. Yet, the avoidant's tendency to keep emotions at bay, like a distant island, can be a puzzle to the secure. The keys to this puzzle? Patience and the openness of words.

Two anxious hearts together can be a storm. Reassurance becomes a demand, a need, and perceived threats ignite intense reactions. Emotions turn into lightning, conflicts thunder. Yet, should they recognize their reflection in each other and use their words effectively, they can navigate their stormy seas towards calmer waters.

An anxious and an avoidant, a challenging dance indeed. The anxious yearns for closeness, craves reassurance. The avoidant seeks space, values independence. A cycle ensues: a push for intimacy, a pull for space, and the anxious' fears of rejection echo louder. Professional help might be the conductor they need, guiding them to the music of better communication and understanding.

And avoidant with avoidant? Emotions kept at arm's length, independence held high. They might respect each other's space, yet their dance may lack the rhythm of emotional depth and intimacy. But communication, like music, can grow slowly, building a bridge towards emotional closeness.

A GUIDE FOR THE ATTACHED IN LOVE

The journey through romantic relationships is a winding road, a complex map marked by the intersections of attachment styles. Navigating this path requires unique tools for each traveler, each relationship.

Those who find themselves securely attached walk this path with confidence. They carry with them the ability to express their deepest thoughts and feelings with honesty. This openness is their compass, guiding them in their interactions with others.

They possess a well of patience, an understanding that is both a gift and a necessity when their partners tread different paths of attachment. In their journey, they strike a balance between their own independence and the intimacy they share with their partner, like two travelers walking side by side yet appreciating the surrounding landscapes in their own unique ways.

Those with an anxious attachment style find their path marked by a persistent undercurrent of worry. They carry with them a toolkit of self-soothing techniques, including mindfulness exercises and meditation, to calm their restless hearts. Their needs and wants are often voiced clearly, yet they strive to temper their search for reassurance. They understand the importance of cultivating trust in their partner's feelings. And when the path becomes too steep, too rocky, they know that professional guidance can help them navigate their journey.

For those with an avoidant attachment style, their path is often marked by a desire for space, for boundaries. They challenge themselves to peel back their layers, to share their feelings and thoughts, even when it might feel like stepping into unfamiliar territory. They learn to recognize their partner's needs for closeness, finding a balance that respects their own need for independence. They draw their boundaries clearly, defining their comfort zones but remaining open to expanding them, like a map unfolding to reveal new paths.

Across these diverse paths, some strategies remain universal. Communication is the traveler's guidebook, a tool that requires clarity in expression and attentiveness in listening. Boundaries are the signposts, defining comfort zones for time spent together, emotional intimacy, and personal space. Trust is the steady compass, nurtured by reliability and consistency, by following through with promises and by showing vulnerability.

When the road becomes too winding, professional help stands as the expert guide, offering strategies and tools tailored to each traveler's needs. A relationship counselor or therapist can provide the needed directions, the suitable tools.

Yet, at the heart of this journey, is the reminder that all travelers are capable of growth and change. With self-awareness, effort, and perhaps some professional guidance, they can learn to navigate their attachment styles, steering their relationships towards healthier, more fulfilling destinations.

Consider Sarah and John, bound by a bond of three years. Their hearts, brimming with secure attachment, beat in the rhythm of open dialogue, a symphony of sentiments and needs. When discord strikes a dissonant note, they reach for understanding, a salve to soothe the friction. Sarah, upon the precipice of a career opportunity in a distant city, found her path intertwined with John's. Their conversation, a dance between individual aspirations and shared affection, bore the hallmark of their secure attachment, a delicate balance between selfhood and togetherness.

In another corner of this vast human stage, we encounter Austin, a soul marked by anxious attachment. His love story with Lisa is often tinted with the hues of worry, misinterpretations painting shadows on their canvas of connection. A delay in Lisa's text response, an evening spent away in the company of friends – such trivialities metamorphose into harbingers of rejection in Austin's eyes. His heart craves constant reassurance, its rhythm faltering in its absence.

Megan's tale sings a different tune, one echoing with the chords of avoidant attachment. Independence is her cherished possession, intimacy a terrain she treads with caution. Callen, her partner, often finds his attempts to scale the heights of emotional depth met with deflection, his desires for a shared future met with hesitations. Megan's boundaries are her fortress, her retreat from an onslaught of overwhelming closeness. A proposition to cohabit might find her retreating, not for lack of affection, but in her quest to preserve her individuality.

In the vortex of avoidant attachment, we find Sam. His heart, a battlefield of conflicting desires, yearns for Alice's closeness while dreading the very intimacy it craves. He is a mariner lost at sea, tossed between jealousy when Alice seeks others' company, and suffocation when their togetherness stretches into eternity. A weekend with Alice might spark a quarrel, a paradoxical response to the overwhelming intimacy he paradoxically seeks and fears.

These vignettes, plucked from the garden of life, serve as mirrors to the multifaceted nature of human attachment. They echo the symphony of love and connection, each note a reflection of our capacity for growth, change, and self-awareness. The language of love, as complex as can be, is a song we all strive to learn, to understand, and to sing harmoniously.

MARKED BY PATTERNS

The patterns of attraction we experience and the dynamics we build in our relationships are influenced by our attachment styles, which may have a considerable impact on the choice of romantic partners. These habits, which were shaped by the very first ties we made in our lives, are deeply ingrained and frequently unconscious. Let's think about each attachment style and how it could affect the choice of a mate.

Secure Attachment

People who have this attachment type are frequently drawn to and attracted to partners who have this style. They promote relationships that are harmonious and healthy by having a positive outlook on both themselves and other people. They are dependable, steady, and emotionally available because they are at ease with both closeness and independence.

Anxious Attachment

People who have an anxious attachment style are drawn to partners who validate their already-held beliefs and opinions on partnerships. Because it echoes their concerns of abandonment and feeds into their desire for certainty, they could be drawn to partners who are emotionally aloof or inconsistent in their devotion. This can cause them to keep looking for partners who aren't really available or attentive to their requirements.

Avoidant Attachment

People with this attachment type could find themselves drawn to partners who are independent and don't require a lot of intimacy or emotional investment. They could also be drawn to fearful people who respect their desire for privacy. Their attraction tendencies are frequently founded on preserving a degree of emotional distance and independence.

Disorganized Attachment

Individuals with this attachment type may have irregular and inconsistent patterns of attraction. They could stay their idea that intimacy causes suffering towards partners who are emotionally absent, while yearning for the closeness they push away.

Self-awareness and reflection are necessary for identifying these tendencies. Consider your relationships from the past and now. Do you notice any patterns of behavior or dynamics? Do your relationships frequently come across as overly needy or emotionally distant? Do you frequently feel smothered or do they appreciate your desire for independence?

Understanding your personal attachment style is also helpful. This knowledge can shed light on why you might be drawn to particular personality types and assist you in making more thoughtful decisions on your future relationships. You might discover that therapy or counseling might assist you in exploring these patterns in a setting of safety and support.

Though they may be entrenched profoundly, these patterns are not unchangeable. It is possible to transition to a more stable attachment type with knowledge and effort, building better connections along the way. We'll learn how to do this with emotional regulation techniques in Chapter 10.

10

WHAT IS POSSIBLE WHEN YOU MASTER YOUR EMOTIONAL REGULATION

Armed With Knowledge, You're In Control

"Managing our emotional life requires mindfulness. It implies becoming aware of the feelings and reactions we have, and learning to navigate them rather than being led by them."

– Jon Kabat-Zinn

EMOTIONAL REGULATION

Emotional regulation refers to the ability to effectively manage and respond to an emotional experience. It involves being aware of and understanding one's emotions, being able to express them appropriately, and being capable of controlling them when necessary. This can mean enhancing, maintaining, or decreasing both positive and negative emotions depending on the context.

Good emotional regulation is a crucial aspect of mental health and well-being. It allows individuals to navigate their emotional experiences in a manner that is socially acceptable, promotes positive social interactions, and helps to achieve personal goals.

People use a variety of strategies to regulate their emotions, some of which are more adaptive or maladaptive than others. For example, adaptive strategies include problem-solving, reappraisal (changing the way one thinks about a situation), and mindfulness, while maladaptive strategies can include suppression, avoidance, or self-blame.

Difficulty with emotional regulation can be seen in a variety of mental health disorders, including depression, anxiety disorders, and personality disorders.

When we are children, we are continually faced with options as we learn to navigate the world. Jude Cassiify writes how childhood is about learning to select responses. These responses are ultimately used to help us, in any given situation, learn to achieve our goals. As children we largely learn these responses from our parents[53] Ross A. Thompson writes:

"On the basis of the socialization practices of parents and other authorities, children acquire emotion schemas that, among other things, guide their predictions of the consequences of expressing various emotions in certain situations...For example, on the basis of the verbal ... and behavioral guidance of socializing agents, they learn the consequences of responding to an aggressive peer by taking revenge, crying, tattling, or asserting themselves. In doing so, they can more thoughtfully evaluate these alternatives in terms of their relative suitability for accomplishing personal goals in particular circumstances."[54]

These ideas are meant to underscore that emotional regulation is all about being adaptive. If, as children, we are able to adapt our emotions to mirror our caregivers; we are just as capable of adapting them to not.

We develop expectations and sensitivities around our partner's, friends and family. We either learn to hide, or to make our emotions clear in every situation throughout life. It is one of the most important and consistent decisions we'll ever have to make! Again and again...

Ross A. Thompson writes that emotional responses and "emotional regulation processes significantly influence the quality, intensity, timing, and dynamic features and thus significantly color emotion experience." [55] Our ability to function depends on how strongly we feel something and has consequences on every area of our life; especially decision making. The goal of emotional regulation is to be adaptive, see the gray in every situation, not the black and white. And ultimately, to reduce suffering.

THE STRATEGY

Start by introspectively examining the situation and recognizing recurring emotional trends.

Pose this question to yourself: What interpretation is being applied to the situation, and what fundamental belief or value does it stimulate?

Search for evidence that contradicts your initial interpretation and mull over it.

Here's an example in practice

Amy was a dedicated employee who always put in her best efforts at work. However, she often found herself in a cycle of stress and anxiety, particularly during team meetings. She noticed a recurring theme: whenever her boss would ask someone else a question or give praise to a colleague, Amy felt overlooked and undervalued.

After recognizing this recurring emotional trend, Amy decided to introspectively examine the situation. She asked herself, "What interpretation am I giving to these situations, and what core belief or value does this feeling tap into?" Amy realized that she equated attention and recognition from her boss with her self-worth and job security.

However, Amy also knew that she was a valued member of the team and that her work was respected. She decided to look for evidence that contradicted her initial interpretation of the situation. She recalled instances when her boss privately commended her work, included her in critical projects, and relied on her expertise.

Amy mulled over this evidence and realized that her initial interpretation might not be entirely accurate. She recognized that meetings were often about collaborative discussion and problem-solving, not personal accolades. Her boss was simply encouraging participation from all members.

This new perspective helped Amy mitigate her stress and anxiety. She learned to separate her self-worth from public recognition, understanding that her value at work wasn't solely defined by the attention she received during meetings. This introspective process allowed Amy to break her recurring emotional trend and foster a healthier interpretation of her work environment.

Understanding this process is beneficial for emotional regulation in the following way:

The act of reflecting on a situation and identifying patterns in your emotional reactions encourages self-awareness. By doing this, you can gain a better understanding of what triggers your emotional responses, and you can begin to anticipate and prepare for these triggers, fostering better emotional control.

Asking yourself about the meaning you assign to a situation and what core beliefs it activates helps you to recognize the impact of your cognitive processes on your emotions. Sometimes, we may assign meaning or interpretations to situations based on our beliefs or past experiences that can heighten emotional responses. By understanding this, we can begin to challenge and change unhelpful thought patterns.

Finally, actively seeking and reflecting on evidence that contradicts your initial interpretation of a situation is a cognitive restructuring technique. It allows you to challenge your perspective and possibly reframe the situation in a less emotionally charged or more positive light. This practice can help reduce intense emotional reactions, promote more balanced emotions, and encourage more adaptive responses to similar situations in the future.

HOW IT WORKS

Imagine, you're grappling with a so-called friend over a duty you both signed up for. Your comrade has abandoned their post, leaving you to wrestle with the task like some solitary soldier in the trenches. But before you succumb to the volcanic eruption building within you, take a step back. Breathe. Swim through the murky waters of your resentment and surface, clutching your patience tightly. Then, with the calm of a low tide, convey your disappointment and burden. You might be surprised to find that this exchange becomes less of a battleground, more of a peace treaty.

Picture this: your beloved keeps disappearing into the labyrinth of their work life, leaving you pacing the home corridors, waiting for a sign of their return. The chill of disrespect and neglect starts creeping in, tempting you to surrender to the anger brewing in your chest. But, don't. Instead, navigate the labyrinth of your own emotions. Unearth the root of your response—could it be fear? Insecurity? Once you've unraveled these threads, approach your partner. Drape your feelings over their shoulders with the softness of a confession, not the harshness of an accusation. Together, chart a new course out of this maze.

Now, imagine the spotlight of critique glaring at you in an office meeting. A colleague dissects your work with the cold precision of a scalpel, leaving you reeling. But don't let your defensiveness transform into a hard shell. Instead, use emotional regulation as a shield. Weigh their criticism on the scales of constructive feedback, and if the balance tilts favorably, accept it. Answer with the grace of a seasoned professional, inviting their guidance rather than their judgment.

Consider the realm of parenthood, a battleground where patience is often the first casualty. Picture your offspring, stubbornly refusing their educational duties. You could let frustration sweep you off your feet, but why not root yourself in emotional regulation instead? Recognize your own irritation, but transform it into a tranquil teaching moment. Explain to your child the value of diligence, offering your guidance instead of your wrath.

In all these situations, you'll see how emotional regulation morphs potential chaos into harmonious resolution. It nurtures thoughtful interactions that respect your own emotional landscape and also acknowledges the contours of the other's.

IMPORTANT PRACTICE

While it might be difficult, maintaining emotional control over time is unquestionably beneficial.

Use relaxation techniques — By reducing feelings of tension and anxiety, techniques like deep breathing, progressive muscle relaxation, and guided imagery you can better control your emotions.

Practice mindfulness — Regular mindfulness practice can assist you in being more conscious of your emotional state. You can recognize when your emotions are about to get out of control so you can act more quickly and wisely when it's necessary.

Create Healthy Habits — Emotional and physical well-being are correlated. Better emotional control can be facilitated by regular exercise, a good diet, enough sleep, and moderate alcohol and caffeine consumption.

Learn coping mechanisms to deal with stress and other adverse situations, emotions. This might involve pastimes, time spent in nature, keeping a journal, or chatting with friends.

In times of stress, don't be afraid to turn to your support system for assistance. Friends, relatives, or support networks can offer a sympathetic ear, words of encouragement, and guidance.

A mental health expert may be able to help you if you regularly feel as though your emotions are out of control or overpowering. Emotional regulation can be greatly improved with the use of dialectical behavior therapy (DBT), cognitive-behavioral therapy (CBT), and other forms of therapy. A specialist may offer tactics and plans made especially for your requirements and situation.

Consistency is Key—Learning and developing emotional management skills takes time. No matter what, be kind to yourself and acknowledge your improvement, how little it could appear.

Emotion Regulation Training—Programs like Emotion Regulation Training are created to provide people tools they may use to better control their emotions.

Keep in mind that experiencing a variety of emotions is perfectly natural and acceptable, and that emotional regulation doesn't include holding back your emotions. Instead, it's about developing healthy emotional management skills that are consistent with your beliefs and enable you to react appropriately to the current circumstance.

Knowing how to emotionall regulate is key to healing your core wounds. We'll delve into the depths of your heart in chapter 11, in order to align your needs and those things that were out of your control; attachment core wounds.

11

RESTORE TRUST BY HEALING YOUR ATTACHMENT WOUND

Rebuilding Bridges

There is no greater journey than the one that you must take to discover all of the mysteries that lie within you.

– Michelle Sandlin

ATTACHMENT WOUNDS

The architecture of the human soul is rooted in a primal hunger for connection; a profound need to weave ourselves into the lives of others. This is a need that is intrinsic and tenacious, embedded in us from the moment of our first breath. As newborns swaddled in soft cloth, we yearn for the comforting touch of another, a desire that evolves but never truly dissipates as we advance through childhood, adolescence, and into the complexity of adulthood. This longing to be seen, to be truly comprehended, to be unconditionally accepted, is far from a fleeting whim. It is the powerful current that shapes our interactions, molds our relationships, and ultimately, sculpts our very being.

Our longing for love is not a passive wish but a clamoring necessity. However, the road towards fulfilling this longing is often strewn with obstacles. Regrettably, our primal need for connection is sometimes left unmet, resulting in wounds that may lie dormant but are far from benign. As time moves us inexorably forward, these old attachment injuries can subtly contort, presenting themselves anew in our adult relationships in a myriad of forms. As such, the labyrinth of human connection is as complex as it is essential, an endless quest towards understanding and acceptance.

Many human emotions hold in their core an attachment wound - a piercing testament to the misalignment of understanding, recognition, and acceptance between a parent and a child. This deep-seated bond, the act of truly 'seeing' another's soul, is not a mere whim of our own hearts. It is a universal cry, an absolute necessity for all humans, and is a lifeline of paramount importance to the youngest among us.

When this need is left unfulfilled, an instinctual protest ensues: the very fibers of our being shift into a state of tension and readiness, the fight-or-flight mechanism of our nervous system taking the reins. But what if this primal defiance does not yield the desired connection? The child may retreat, severing the cord to this unmet need. A silent message begins to engrave itself on their tender psyche: that they are insignificant, or unworthy of acknowledgment.

The articulation of this deeply embedded message is often beyond the capacity of the child, transcending verbal expression or immediate intellectual comprehension. Yet, it is an experience that permeates their consciousness, a feeling that rings true in the silent chambers of their heart. As the sands of time slip through the hourglass, and if the landscape of their upbringing is marred by continuous neglect, or worse, marred by toxicity and abuse, these unhealthy messages calcify into core beliefs. They become internal monologues about their self-worth and understanding of relationships, shaping the lens through which they view their world.

REPAIRING YOUR ATTACHMENT WOUNDS

Our biological machinery, the complex nexus of nerves that govern our existence, is intrinsically attuned to disruptions in our relationships - the chords of attachment that bind us to those we cherish. This response is born of our innate dependence on the security and connection that these relationships offer for survival. As such, a young, malleable mind can be profoundly influenced by a parent who fails to attend to crucial moments, is lost in their own whirlpool of issues, or is emotionally absent in other capacities. Simply put, it is a lack of acknowledgment or validation of the child's experiences.

The triggering of our body's primary defensive mechanisms - fight, flight, or freeze - is often the result of feeling endangered within these relationships. If the equilibrium of our biological systems remains perpetually disrupted due to persistent exposure to the same disquieting environment, marked by the same parents and the same home, the reality of our unfulfilled needs gives rise to systemic dysregulation. The biological machinery, in a bid to shield us, remains entrenched in these dysregulated states.

Trauma need not necessarily be associated with a discernible event, nor does it imply a parent's inherent malevolence. It merely highlights the parent's inability to resonate emotionally, to grasp the essence of the child's internal universe. Persistent failures in this domain can culminate in the genesis of developmental or attachment traumas, inflicting wounds that persist over time. The child, through a deeply felt, non-verbal understanding, comes to the realization that the relationship they rely on for survival is unreliable. It is at this juncture that their sense of safety evaporates and the body's primal responses - fight, flight, or freeze - are ignited.

This elucidates why children may display disconnection or disruptive behaviors as survival strategies, given that their fundamental needs are not being met. It also explains the complexities faced in adult relationships. While we have outgrown our childhood, the resonating echo of these past experiences can be easily roused, provoking protective behaviors that may have been pertinent in the past, but are detrimental to our present relationships. The crux lies in the realization that as adults, we may be ensconced in safety, and our relationship partners are likely capable and inclined to cater to our needs for connection and intimacy. However, the protective mechanisms ingrained in us can be triggered in intimate moments, prompting us to revert to our old coping mechanisms of disconnection, fight or flight responses, and emotional retreat. Our system's inherent threat detector, calibrated by past experiences, perceives potential danger even in the absence of an actual threat.[56]

THREE STEPS TO HEALING

This process is repeated and expanded in your Workbook with prompts to carefully guide you through this powerful sequence of revelations.

Observation

Could the younger self disclose its burden? We yearn for this past facet of us to reveal what it endured. Consider an instance: "The memories from my childhood, especially the painful divorce of my parents, and the resulting days of hunger I endured with my mother, are agonizing." What narratives are you carrying? From where did the notion of being unlovable originate?

Allow your younger self to reveal its burden to those you trust. What emotions are you grappling with? Is there a persistent sense of doom, fear, anxiety, or melancholy? Where does the discomfort reside? Where are your memories stored, and what emotions do they elicit?

There's someone who is eager to listen to your narrative, be it a therapist or a trusted companion. They desire to bear witness to your journey, and ultimately, you should be willing to observe yourself.

Remedial Experience

This process is internal. Can you offer yourself the affection that others failed to provide? What does your younger self crave? A gentle peck on the forehead? A reassuring whisper that all will be well? Your companions and partners can embody this role for you as well. The younger self first discloses its burden, then imparts what it has learned, and eventually receives what it requires. Doctor Frank Anderson asserts that this entire process is feasible within our imagination and, in fact, beneficial to our brains, given the immense neuroplasticity harbored within our imaginative realms.[57]

Release And Transformation

According to Dr. Anderson, once the afflicted aspect is "acknowledged, empathized with, and comprehended, once a remedial experience has occurred, then it's empowered to relinquish its burden." Upon understanding your inner self and the depths of the burden you bear, you're able to set free the pain that has been shackled to your being. The experience need not be an enduring burden, and you are then granted the liberty to let go.

FORGIVENESS

In the quest to mend attachment wounds, forgiveness emerges as a pivotal component. It's frequently likened to the emancipation of a captive, only to realize that the captive was in fact, oneself. This analogy holds substantial relevance when addressing attachment wounds. By embracing forgiveness, we free ourselves from the chains of past trauma, thereby paving the way for recovery and personal development.

Forgiveness operates as a powerful instrument in the repair of these emotional scars. By extending forgiveness to those who have caused us pain—our friends, caregivers, and most importantly, ourselves—we disrupt the perpetual cycle of accusation and suffering that binds us to our wounds. It feels akin to sketching a definitive boundary around our past, demarcating a distinct separation between the torment of what has been and the potential for healing that lies ahead.

Forgiveness does not mean forgetting or condoning harmful behavior; rather, it is an act of self-care, a commitment to our own emotional well-being. It allows us to reclaim our narrative, to rewrite our story from one of hurt to one of healing and resilience. Forgiving others—our friends and caregivers who may have been unable, for whatever reason, to meet our needs fully—can release us from the bitterness and resentment that keep our wounds raw.

Perhaps more challenging, but no less crucial, is the practice of self-forgiveness. Many people carry guilt or shame from past experiences, blaming themselves for not acting differently, for not being able to change the situation. Yet, self-forgiveness invites us to understand and accept our human limitations. Recognizing that we, too, were navigating challenging circumstances to the best of our abilities allows us to release self-judgment and open ourselves to self-compassion, which is a powerful salve for attachment wounds.

Nevertheless, it's essential to acknowledge that forgiveness is not an event, but a process. It is complicated, multi-layered, and different for everyone. Some find it easier to forgive others than to forgive themselves. For others, the opposite is true. The journey toward forgiveness may be fraught with resistance and relapses into old patterns of resentment and self-blame. It requires patience, perseverance, and, most importantly, the gentle acknowledgment that progress does not always follow a linear path.

In truth, forgiveness can be a profoundly challenging part of the healing process. It may require the support of therapeutic interventions or the empathy of friends who can walk alongside us in our journey. But in its heart, forgiveness is a journey towards freedom—a crucial step towards repairing attachment wounds, embracing healing, and moving forward.

REPAIRED

Grasping the mechanisms of mending attachment injuries and enhancing interpersonal connections can be daunting, but tangible life instances frequently illuminate this profound process of transformation.

There are many examples we can draw from, or take a page from their book if you will.

Michael Phelps, a renowned Olympian with an impressive array of accolades, has candidly spoken about his battles with mental health challenges connected to his formative years and various pressures. His path towards remedying these deep-seated emotional injuries heavily involved therapy, particularly cognitive behavioral therapy. This therapeutic intervention played a pivotal role in helping him foster more wholesome personal and career-related relationships.

The esteemed actor Keanu Reeves has been acquainted with substantial grief and difficulties from an early age, conditions that could cultivate attachment wounds. Notwithstanding these tribulations, Reeves has succeeded in establishing a thriving career and nurturing enduring relationships. His tenacity presents a moving testament to the capacity for recovery and development, even in the face of profound traumas.

Maya Angelou. The late poet and civil rights activist had a traumatic childhood, with experiences that led to deep emotional wounds. Yet, she managed to heal over time, using her voice and her writing as tools of resilience. Her life and work continue to inspire many in their own journeys of healing and personal growth.

As we wrap up this chapter, we affirm the substantial impact of attachment wounds on our existence. Healing might not follow a straight path or happen rapidly, but it remains within our reach. The narratives we've shared and the wisdom we've garnered illuminate that self-love, forgiveness, and the courage to request assistance form the cornerstone of this journey. Our past does not confine us; instead, it offers lessons for growth and transcendence beyond our emotional injuries. In our subsequent chapter, we will delve into the specific methods and tools that aid in sparking this transformative healing, offering a compass to navigate towards healthier, more secure relational bonds. You're well on your way!

12

CONCLUSION

What To Do Now

Knowledge without application is like a book that is never opened; it holds immense potential, but its true value remains untapped.

– Christopher Crawford

As we bring this journey through the fascinating landscape of attachment theory to a close, we reflect upon the insightful exploration of our attachment styles—whether secure, anxious, avoidant, or disorganized. Each style, a map of our emotional history, offers us invaluable insights into our relational patterns. This understanding allows us to identify our core wounds and work towards healing them, promoting growth and evolution in our relationships.

The incorporation of mindfulness throughout this transformative journey helps us remain present, observing our feelings, reactions, and triggers without judgment. This conscious awareness enables us to understand our patterns, paving the way for significant change.

Remember, attachment styles are not fixed imprints but fluid and malleable. Throughout our lives, they can shift and change based on experiences, personal growth, and healing. While we may have been influenced by our early relationships, the goal of achieving secure attachment remains within our reach. As we continue to heal and grow, we shape our relational world, fostering secure, healthy bonds.

This exploration of attachment theory empowers us with self-awareness and hope. The understanding that we are not bound by our past, but can change and secure healthier, fulfilling relationships, illuminates our path forward.

As we reach the end of our exploration into attachment theory, it's crucial to take a moment to reflect on the journey we have undertaken. Each chapter, complemented by the Workbook, has been designed not only to enlighten but to empower and equip you with tools to revolutionize your relationships.

Chapter One served as a mirror, reflecting the recurring patterns within your relationships and shedding light on their origin. It prompted the essential question: Why do all your relationships end up the same? Understanding that these patterns are deeply rooted in your attachment style was the first step on this transformative path.

In Chapter Two, we delved into the origins of your attachment style and the core wounds associated with it. The influence of early-life experiences and interactions with primary caregivers became evident, highlighting how these formative moments shape our relational landscapes.

Chapter Three introduced the four primary ways of being in a relationship—secure, anxious, avoidant, and disorganized—each with its unique characteristics, challenges, and ways of relating to others. These categories offered a more nuanced understanding of your attachment style, a crucial foundation for the following chapters.

Chapters Four through Seven went in-depth into each attachment style. The exploration began with the secure attachment style in Chapter Four, followed by avoidant, anxious, and disorganized attachment styles in the subsequent chapters. These sections illuminated each style's unique facets and coping mechanisms, providing a deeper understanding of your relational tendencies.

In Chapter Eight, you began to harness your newfound knowledge to transform your relationships. Recognizing the influence of your attachment style on your relationships was pivotal in beginning the process of change.

Chapter Nine centered on how to attract and sustain the love you desire, with emphasis on the importance of open communication, vulnerability, and respect for boundaries.

Chapter Ten provided practical tools for emotional regulation, essential skills for managing relationship stress and navigating difficult emotions. These tools can be a lifeline in challenging situations, allowing you to respond rather than react.

Chapter Eleven guided you through the healing process, offering strategies to mend your attachment wounds. This chapter shed light on the role of self-care, forgiveness, and re-framing experiences in overcoming attachment-related challenges.

Finally, this, Chapter Twelve served as a culmination of all the insights gained throughout the book.

The accompanying Workbook is an invaluable tool throughout this journey, allowing you to put theory into practice, reinforce the insights gained, and track your progress.

Finally, remember that understanding is just the first step. Real transformation requires time, patience, and consistent effort. Use the tools and insights you've gained to revolutionize your relationships, and remember that healing and growth are lifelong journeys. This exploration of attachment theory is not an end, but rather a new beginning, a stepping stone towards healthier, happier, and more fulfilling relationships.

IN 90 SECONDS YOU CAN MAKE A HUGE DIFFERENCE

If you feel we've deserved it, please take a moment to leave a review on Amazon.

Your feedback means the world to us. It helps us to improve and it means better learning experiences for all our readers.

We'd be so grateful to you for your review!

Thank you!
Thank you!
Thank you!

REFERENCES

1. https://www.amazon.com/s?k=notes+from+your+therapist
&hvadid=486277614884&hvdev=c&hvlocphy=9067609&hvn
etw=g&hvqmt=e&hvrand=17426368229358453361&hvtargid
=kwd-1077961811436&hydadcr=27889_10745035&tag=goog
hydr-20&ref=pd_sl_8evpxeansx_e

2. https://www.attachmentproject.com/blog/secure-attachment/

3. https://www.attachmentproject.com/attachment-theory/

4. Ainsworth, M. D. S., Wittig, B. A. (1969). Attachment and the exploratory behavior of one-year-olds in a strange situation. In B. M. Foss (Ed.), Determinants of infant behavior (Vol. 4, pp. 113-136). London: Methuen.

5. Bretherton, I. (1992). The origins of attachment theory: John Bowlby and Mary Ainsworth. Developmental Psychology, 28(5), 759–775

6. Ainsworth, M. D. S., Blehar, M. C, Waters, E., Wall, S. (1978). Patterns of attachment: A psychological study of the strange situation. Hillsdale, NJ: Erlbaum

7. Ainsworth, M. D. S., Blehar, M. C, Waters, E., Wall, S. (1978). Patterns of attachment: A psychological study of the strange situation. Hillsdale, NJ: Erlbaum

8. https://www.parentingforbrain.com/strange-situation/

9. https://www.attachmentproject.com/attachment-theory/

10. BOLEN, R. M. (2000). VALIDITY OF ATTACHMENT THEORY. Trauma, Violence & Abuse, 1(2), 128–153. http://www.jstor.org/stable/26636245

11. Hazan, C., & Shaver, P. R. (1994). Deeper into Attachment Theory. Psychological Inquiry, 5(1), 68–79. http://www.jstor.org/stable/1449089

12. https://www.verywellmind.com/what-is-attachment-theory-2795337

13. BOLEN, R. M. (2000). VALIDITY OF ATTACHMENT THEORY. Trauma, Violence & Abuse, 1(2), 128–153. http://www.jstor.org/stable/26636245

14. http://www.traumatys.com/wp-content/uploads/2017/09/Dynamic-Bowlby-A-Secure-Base-Clinical-Applications-1988-1.pdf

15. http://www.traumatys.com/wp-content/uploads/2017/09/Dynamic-Bowlby-A-Secure-Base-Clinical-Applications-1988-1.pdf

16. http://www.traumatys.com/wp-content/uploads/2017/09/Dynamic-Bowlby-A-Secure-Base-Clinical-Applications-1988-1.pdf

17. http://www.traumatys.com/wp-content/uploads/2017/09/Dynamic-Bowlby-A-Secure-Base-Clinical-Applications-1988-1.pdf

18. http://www.traumatys.com/wp-content/uploads/2017/09/Dynamic-Bowlby-A-Secure-Base-Clinical-Applications-1988-1.pdf

19. BOLEN, R. M. (2000). VALIDITY OF ATTACHMENT THEORY. Trauma, Violence & Abuse, 1(2), 128–153. http://www.jstor.org/stable/26636245

20. BOLEN, R. M. (2000). VALIDITY OF ATTACHMENT THEORY. Trauma, Violence & Abuse, 1(2), 128–153. http://www.jstor.org/stable/26636245

21. https://www.washingtonpost.com/news/soloish/wp/2018/08/16/knowing-your-attachment-style-could-make-you-a-smarter-dater/

22. https://pubmed.ncbi.nlm.nih.gov/26213376/

23. https://pubmed.ncbi.nlm.nih.gov/27603938/

24. Bukowski, H., Boch, M., Lamm, C., & Silani, G. (2020). Is Self-Other distinction malleable? Egocentric and altercentric biases in empathy are modulated by priming attachment style and similarity mindsets.

25. Konieczny P, Cierpiałkowska L. Positive and negative life experiences and changes in internal working models of attachment - a comparative study. Psychiatr Pol. 2022 Jun 30;56(3):551-570. English, Polish. doi: 10.12740/PP/OnlineFirst/127457. Epub 2022 Jun 30. PMID: 36342985.

26. Volling, B. L., Notaro, P. C., & Larsen, J. J. (1998). Adult Attachment Styles: Relations with Emotional Well-Being, Marriage, and Parenting. Family Relations, 47(4), 355–367. https://doi.org/10.2307/585266

27. Cohn, D.A., Silver, D.H., Cowan, C.P., Cowan, P.A., & Pearson, J.L. (1992). Working Models of Childhood Attachment and Couple Relationships. Journal of Family Issues, 13, 432 - 449.

28. Owino, W.O., Asakhulu, N.M., Mwania, J.M., & Mwanza, R. (2021). ATTACHMENT STYLES AND RISKY SEXUAL BEHAVIORS IN ADOLESCENTS. Problems of Education in the 21st Century.

29. Volling, B. L., Notaro, P. C., & Larsen, J. J. (1998). Adult Attachment Styles: Relations with Emotional Well-Being, Marriage, and Parenting. Family Relations, 47(4), 355–367. https://doi.org/10.2307/585266

30. Kanninen, K.M., Punamäki, R., & Qouta, S.R. (2003). Personality and Trauma: Adult Attachment and Posttraumatic Distress Among Former Political Prisoners. Peace and Conflict: Journal of Peace Psychology, 9, 97-126.

31. Joseph, M. A., O'Connor, T. G., Briskman, J. A., Maughan, B., & Scott, S. (2014). The formation of secure new attachments by children who were maltreated: an observational study of adolescents in foster care. Development and psychopathology, 26(1), 67–80. https://doi.org/10.1017/S0954579413000540

32. Ensink, K., Fonagy, P., Normandin, L., Rozenberg, A., Marquez, C., Godbout, N., & Borelli, J. L. (2021). Post-traumatic Stress Disorder in Sexually Abused Children: Secure Attachment as a Protective Factor. Frontiers in psychology, 12, 646680. https://doi.org/10.3389/fpsyg.2021.646680

33. Joseph, M. A., O'Connor, T. G., Briskman, J. A., Maughan, B., & Scott, S. (2014). The formation of secure new attachments by children who were maltreated: an observational study of adolescents in foster care. Development and psychopathology, 26(1), 67–80. https://doi.org/10.1017/S0954579413000540

34. https://books.google.com/books/about/Attachment_Theory.html?id=vYl2yAEACAAJ

35. https://www.attachmentproject.com/blog/avoidant-attachment-style/

36. Volling, B. L., Notaro, P. C., & Larsen, J. J. (1998). Adult Attachment Styles: Relations with Emotional Well-Being, Marriage, and Parenting. Family Relations, 47(4), 355–367. https://doi.org/10.2307/585266

37. Volling, B. L., Notaro, P. C., & Larsen, J. J. (1998). Adult Attachment Styles: Relations with Emotional Well-Being, Marriage, and Parenting. Family Relations, 47(4), 355–367. https://doi.org/10.2307/585266

38. https://www.attachmentproject.com/blog/avoidant-attachment-style/

39. https://www.attachmentproject.com/blog/dismissive-avoidant-attachment-superpowers/

40. Linehan, M. M. (2015). DBT skills manual.

41. https://books.google.com/books/about/Attachment_Theory.html?id=vYl2yAEACAAJ

42. https://www.attachmentproject.com/blog/anxious-attachment/

43. https://positivepsychology.com/act-acceptance-and-commitment-therapy/

44. Bellino, S., Brunetti, C., & Bozzatello, P. (2016). La psicoterapia del disturbo borderline di personalità: aspetti critici e proposte terapeutiche [Psychotherapy of borderline personality disorder: critical factors and proposals of intervention]. Rivista di psichiatria, 51(1), 11–19. https://doi.org/10.1708/2168.23446

45. Imperatori, C., Adenzato, M., Palmiero, L., Farina, B., & Ardito, R. B. (2022). Assessment of Unresolved/Disorganized State of Mind in Relation to Attachment: A ROC Curve Study Using the Adult Attachment Interview and the Measure of Parental Style. Clinical neuropsychiatry, 19(4), 197–205. https://doi.org/10.36131/cnfioritieditore20220402

46. Li, Y. (2023). How does attachment style influence early childhood development. Journal of Education, Humanities and Social Sciences.

47. Stinson, P.K. (2016). Running head: ACCOUNTING FOR VARYING ATTACHMENT PRESENTATIONS Accounting for Varying Attachment Presentations: A Limited Literature Review.

48. Li, Y. (2023). How does attachment style influence early childhood development. Journal of Education, Humanities and Social Sciences.

49.   Daniel, S.I. (2014). Adult Attachment Patterns in a
      Treatment Context: Relationship and narrative.

50.   49. B https://books.google.com/books/about/Attachment_
      Theory.html?id=vYl2yAEACAAJ

51.   Iwaniec, D., & Sneddon, H. (2001). Attachment Style in
      Adults who Failed to Thrive as Children: Outcomes
      of a 20 Year Follow-up Study of Factors Influencing
      Maintenance or Change in Attachment Style. The British
      Journal of Social Work, 31(2), 179–195. http://www.jstor.org/
      stable/23716298

52.   Iwaniec, D., & Sneddon, H. (2001). Attachment Style in
      Adults who Failed to Thrive as Children: Outcomes
      of a 20 Year Follow-up Study of Factors Influencing
      Maintenance or Change in Attachment Style. The British
      Journal of Social Work, 31(2), 179–195. http://www.jstor.org/
      stable/23716298

53.   Iwaniec, D., & Sneddon, H. (2001). Attachment Style in
      Adults who Failed to Thrive as Children: Outcomes
      of a 20 Year Follow-up Study of Factors Influencing
      Maintenance or Change in Attachment Style. The British
      Journal of Social Work, 31(2), 179–195. http://www.jstor.org/
      stable/23716298

54.   Cassidy, J. (1994). Emotion Regulation: Influences of
      Attachment Relationships. Monographs of the Society for
      Research in Child Development, 59(2/3), 228–249. https://
      doi.org/10.2307/1166148

55.   Thompson, R. A. (1994). Emotion Regulation: A Theme
      in Search of Definition. Monographs of the Society for
      Research in Child Development, 59(2/3), 25–52. https://doi.
      org/10.2307/1166137

56.   Thompson, R. A. (1994). Emotion Regulation: A Theme
      in Search of Definition. Monographs of the Society for

Research in Child Development, 59(2/3), 25–52. https://doi.org/10.2307/1166137

57. https://www.herosjourneytherapy.com/post/attachment-wounds-yes-you-have-one

58. https://www.herosjourneytherapy.com/post/attachment-wounds-yes-you-have-one

Made in United States
Orlando, FL
14 May 2024

46882356R00088